MW01000710

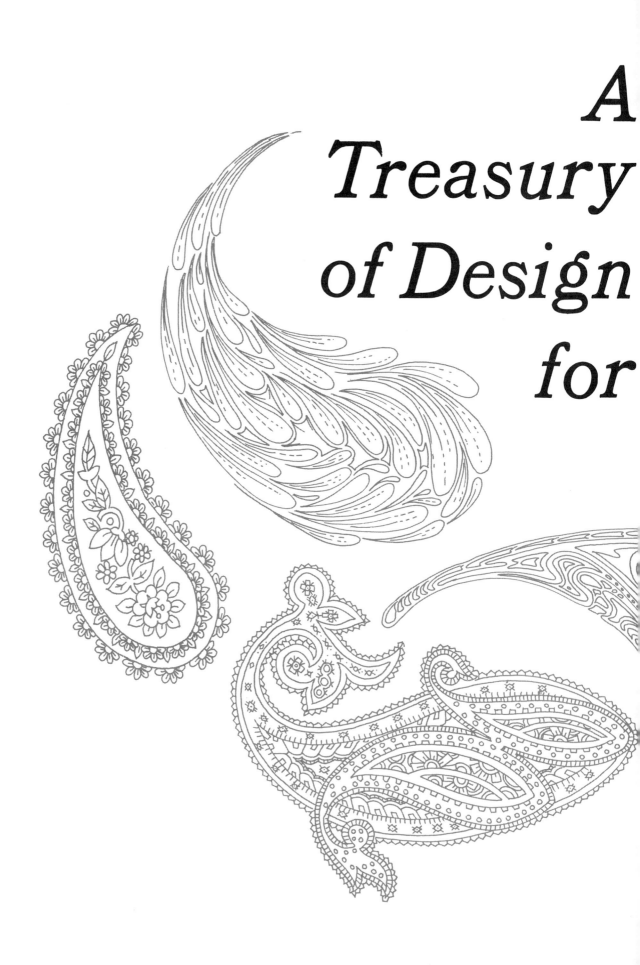

A
Treasury
of Design
for

DOVER *Pictorial Archive* SERIES

Artists
and Craftsmen

725 paisleys, florals, geometrics, folk and primitive motifs

by Gregory Mirow

Dover Publications, Inc.
New York

Published in Canada by General Publishing Company, Ltd.,
30 Lesmill Road, Don Mills, Toronto, Ontario.
Published in the United Kingdom by Constable and Company, Ltd.

DOVER *Pictorial Archive* SERIES

International Standard Book Number: 0-486-22002-8
Library of Congress Catalog Card Number: 69-18877

Manufactured in the United States of America
Dover Publications, Inc.
31 East 2nd Street, Mineola, N.Y. 11501

*Dedicated to my
mother and father*

Contents

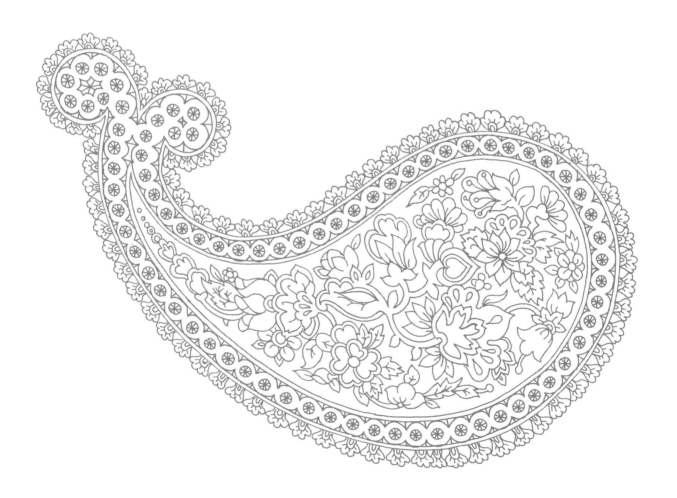

Florals

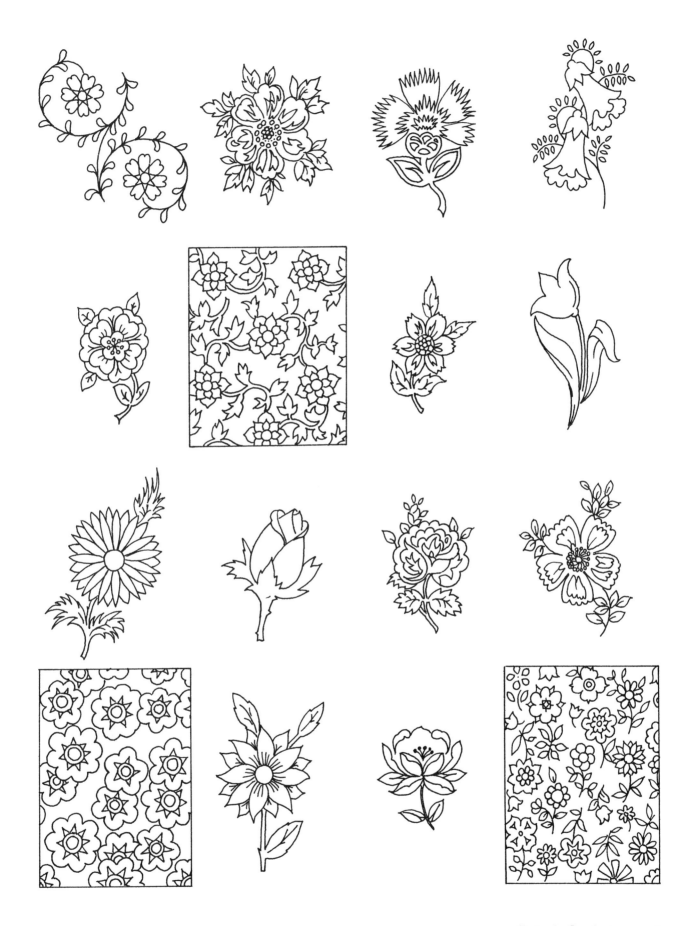

small single florals / PLATE 1

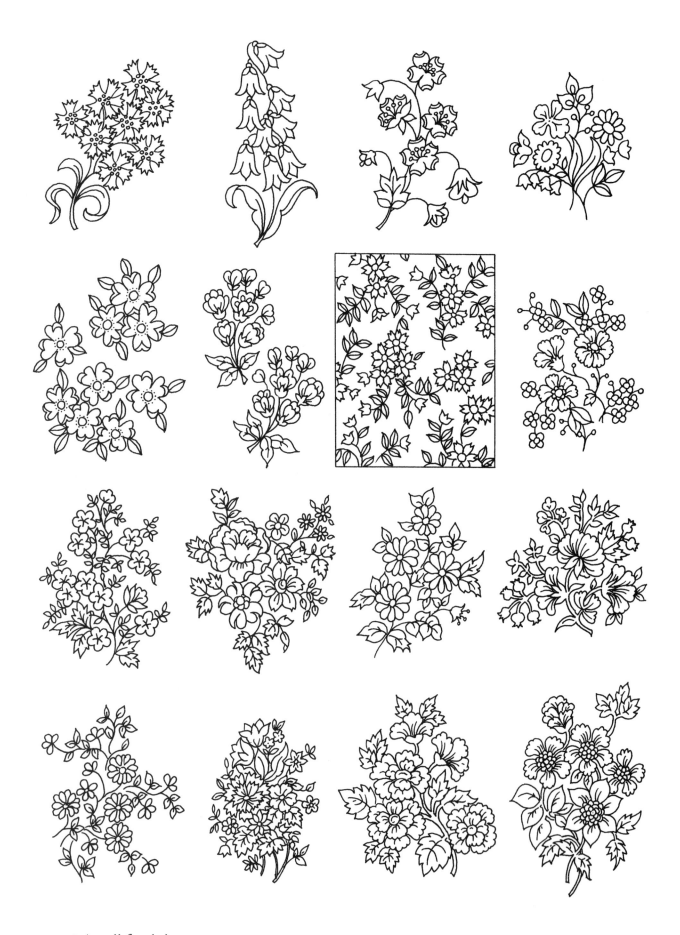

PLATE 2 / small floral clusters

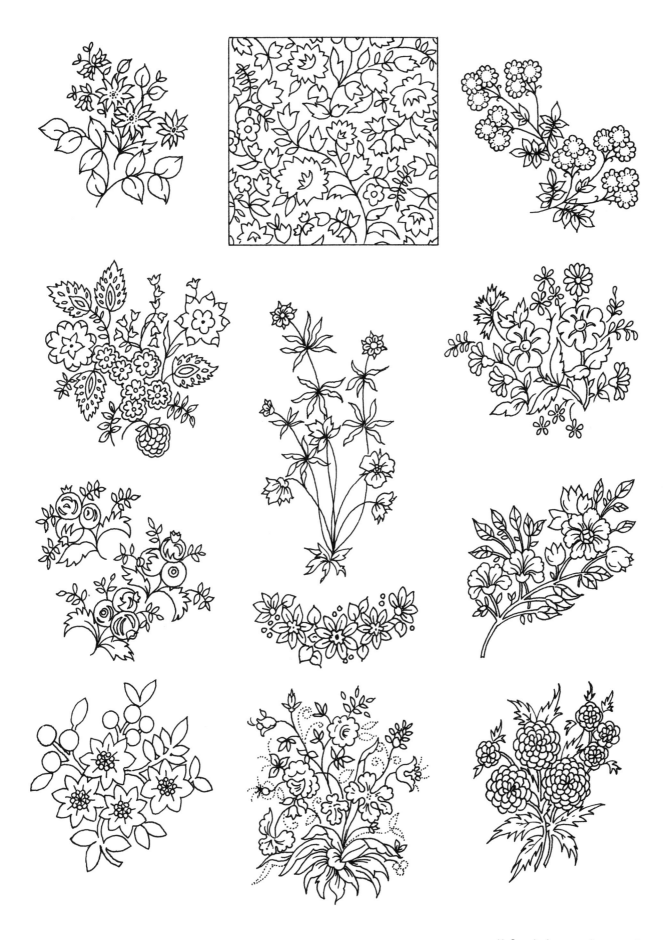

small floral clusters / PLATE 3

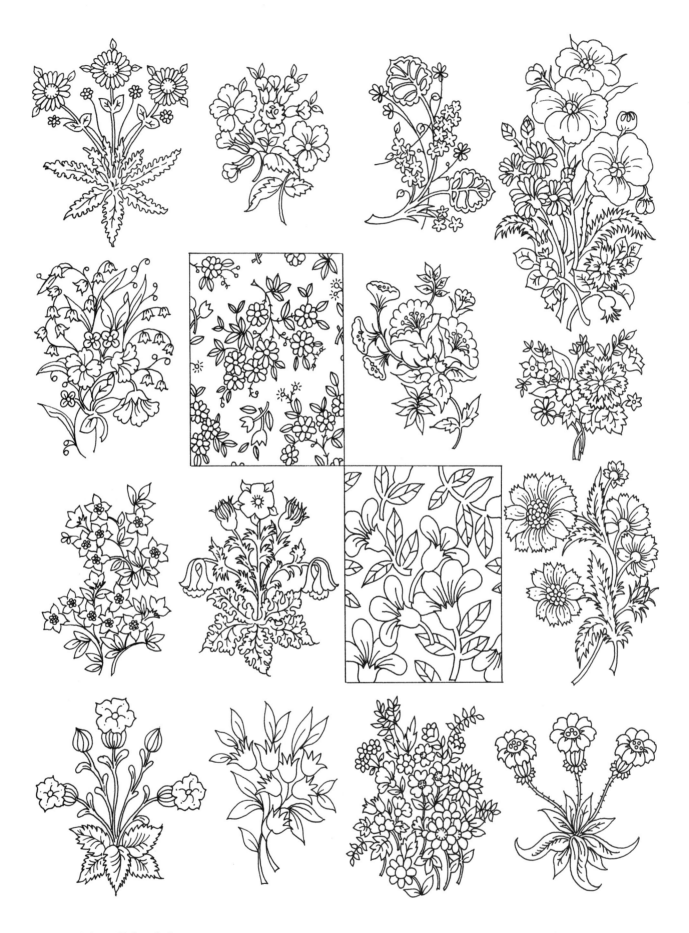

PLATE 4 / small floral clusters

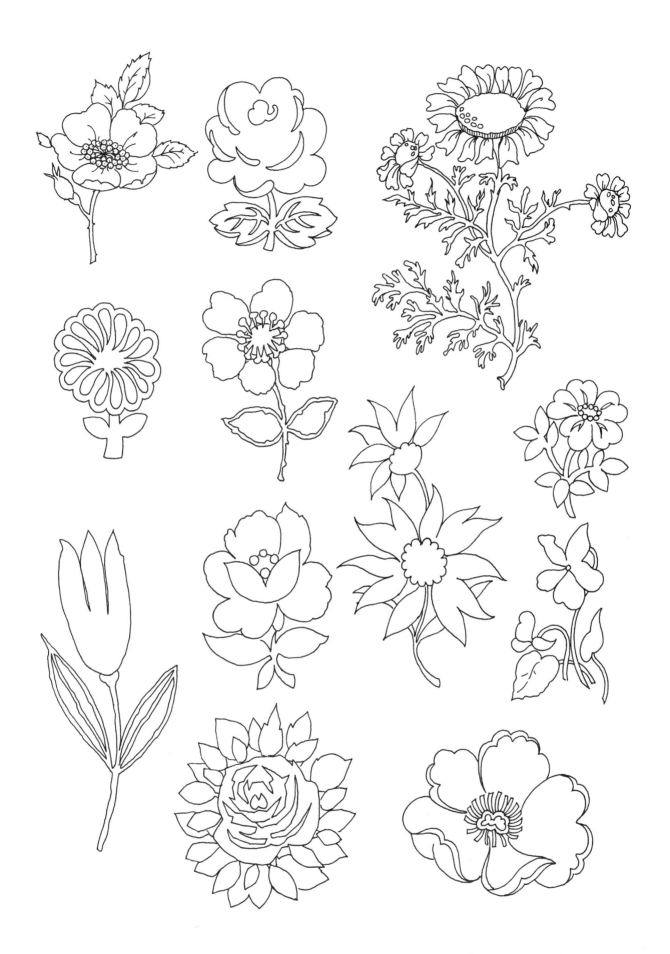

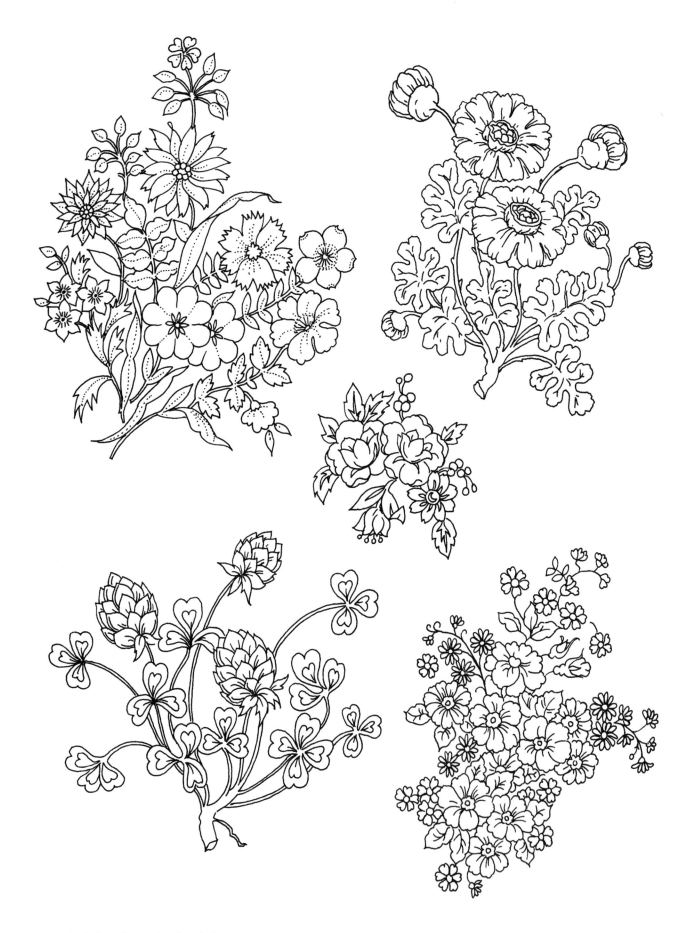

PLATE 6 / medium-size floral clusters

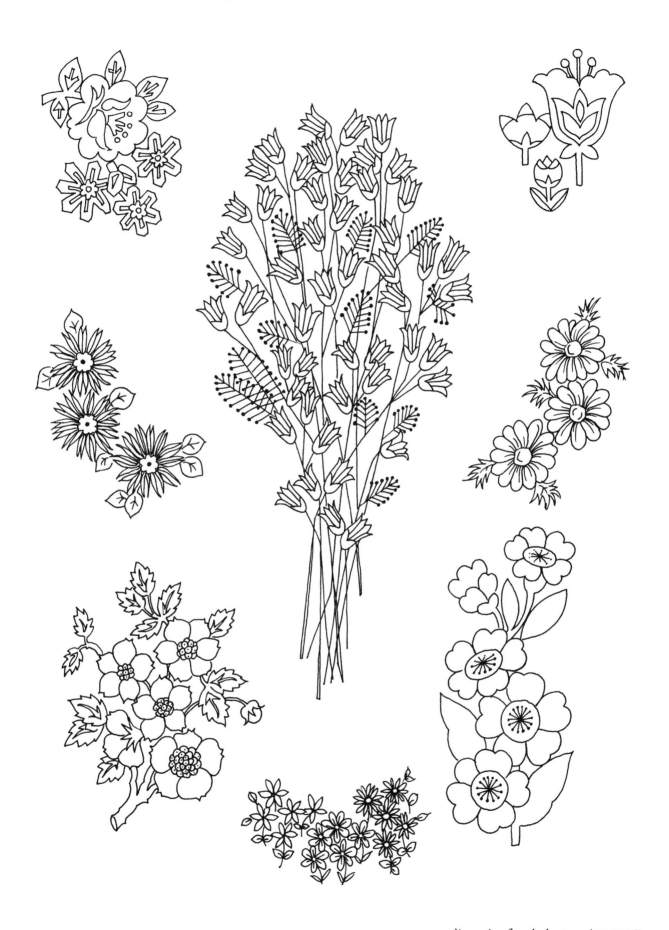

medium-size floral clusters / PLATE 7

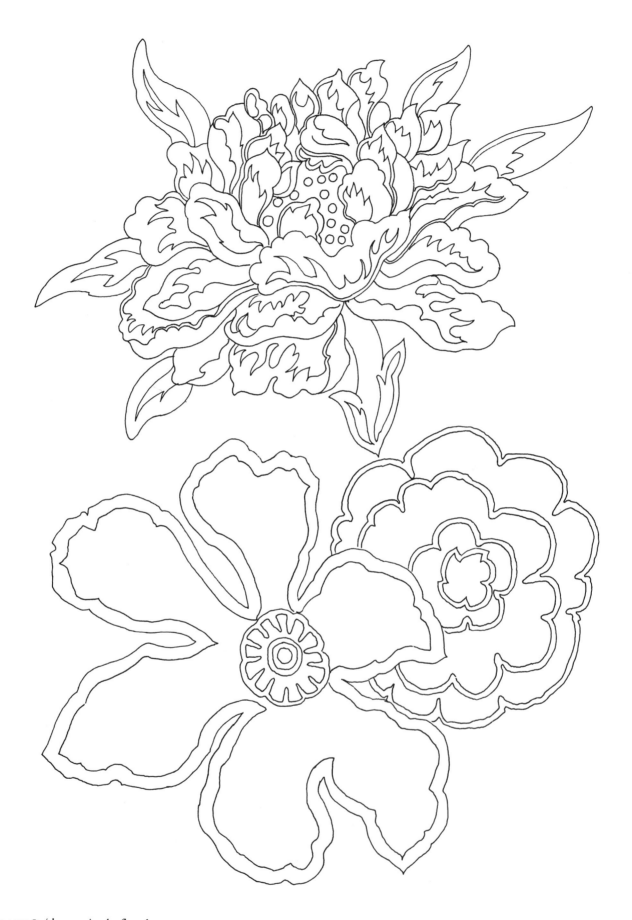

PLATE 8 / large single florals

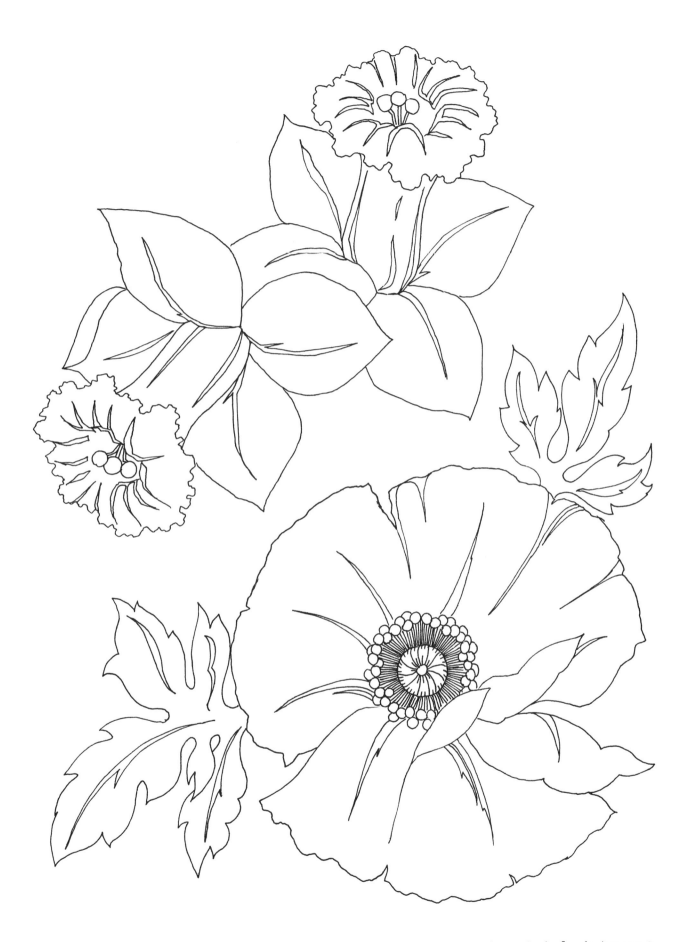

large single florals / PLATE 9

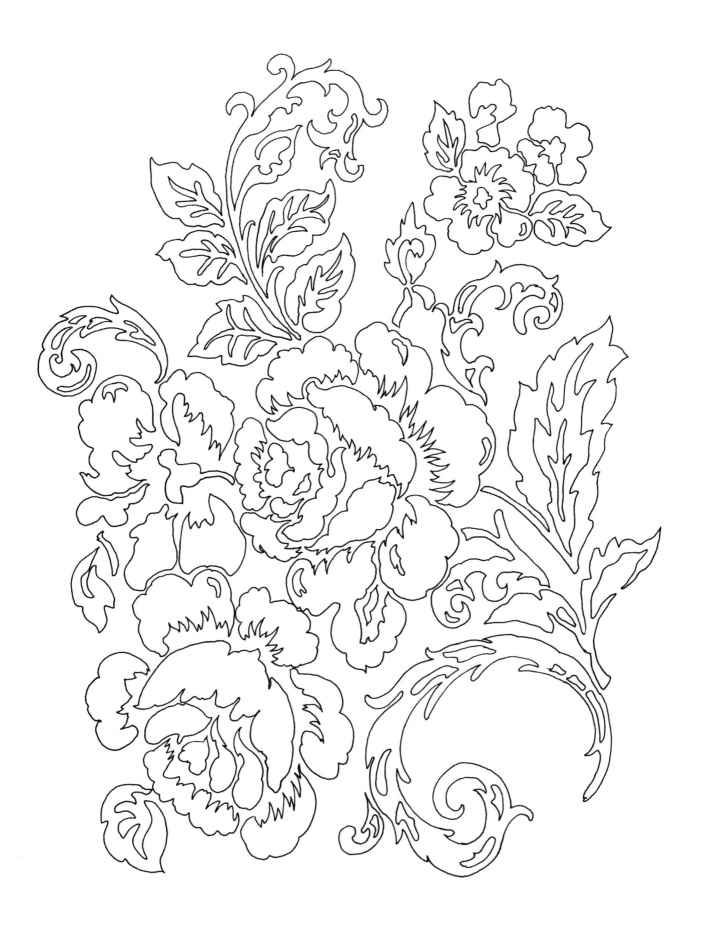

PLATE 10 / large floral cluster

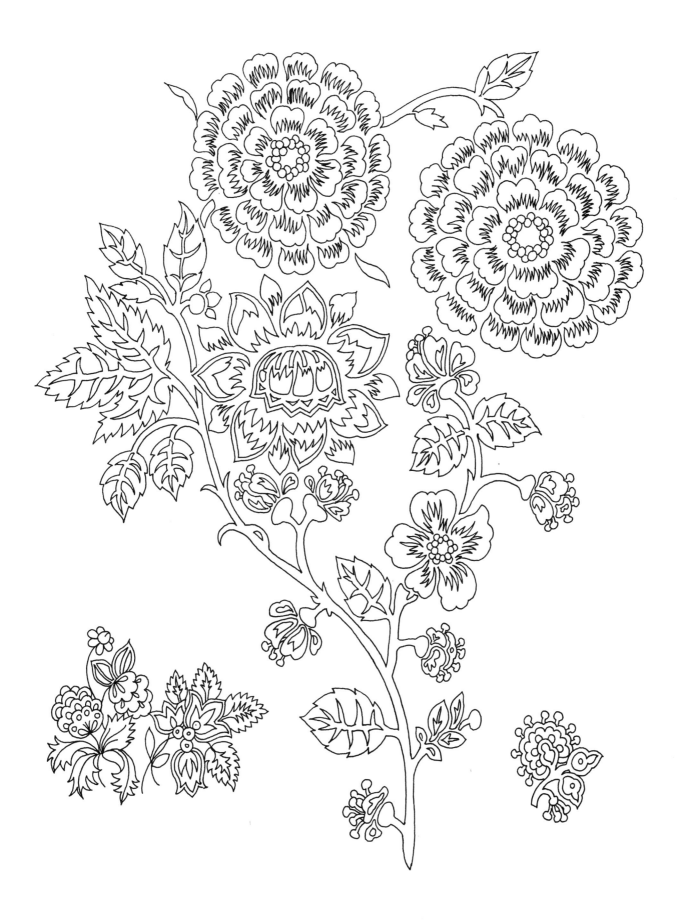

Early American florals / PLATE 11

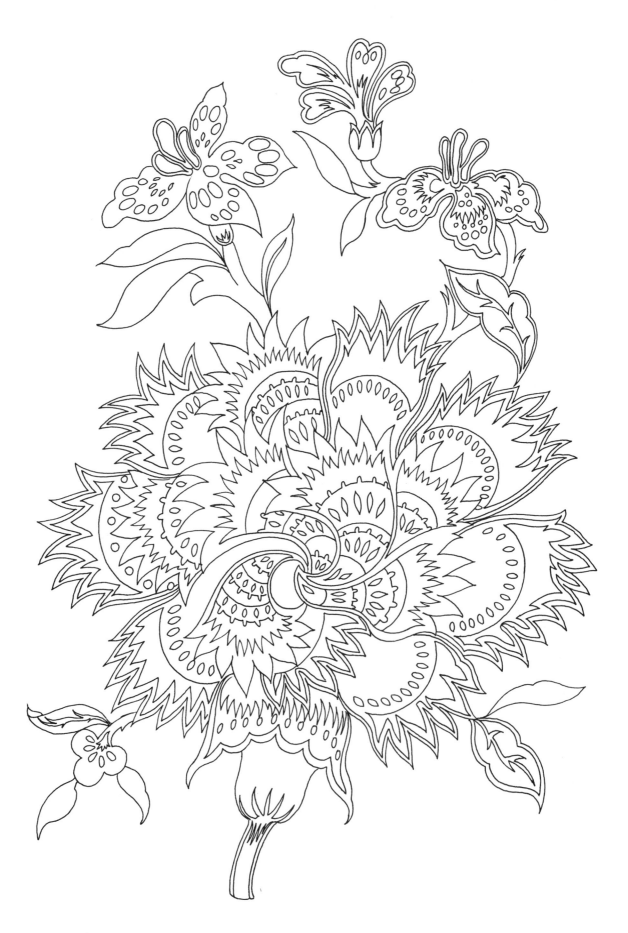

PLATE 12 / Early American floral

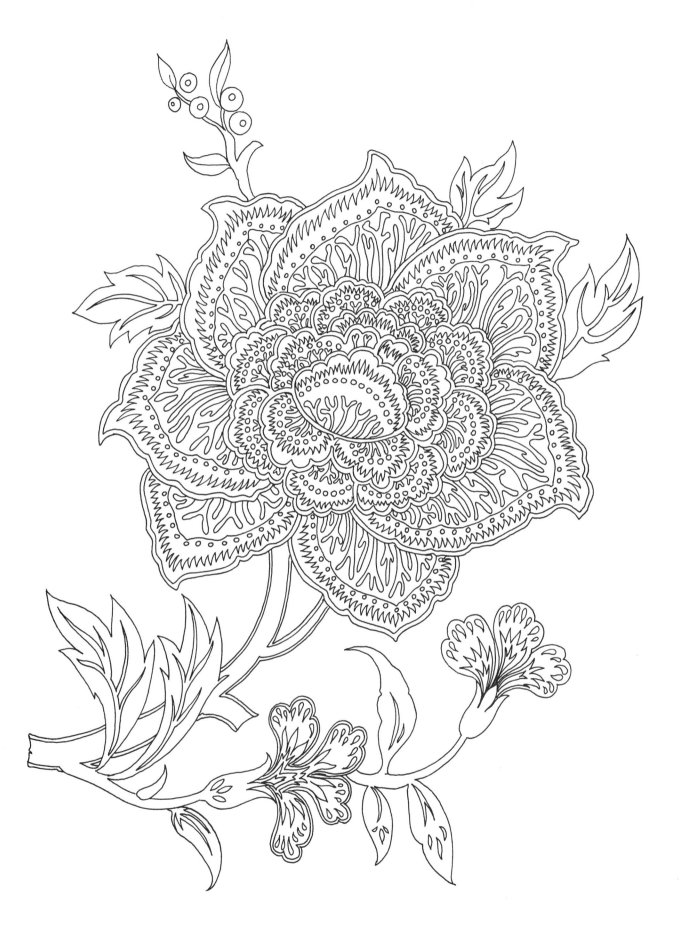

Early American floral / PLATE 13

PLATE 14 / Provincial florals

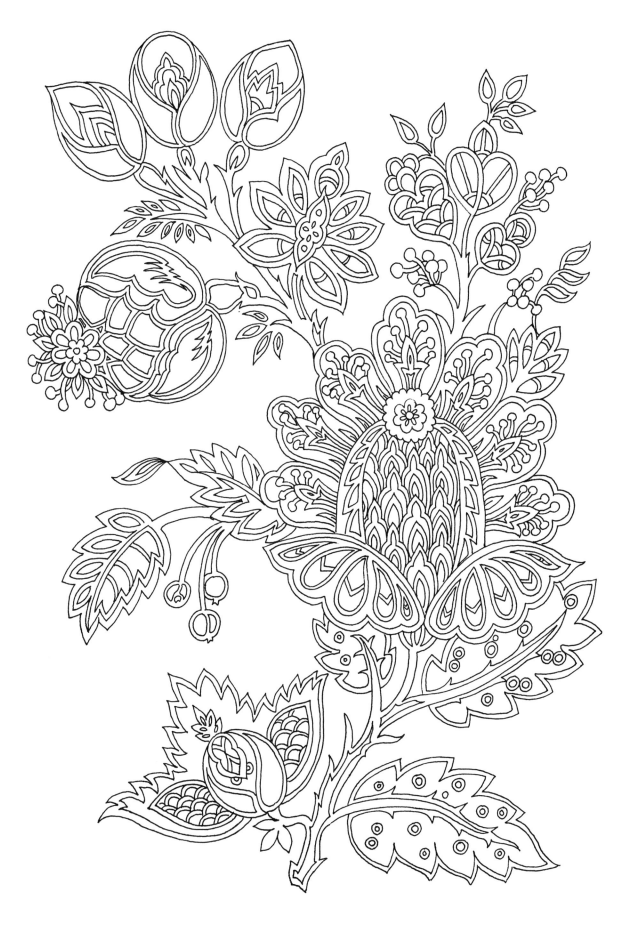

Provincial florals / PLATE 15

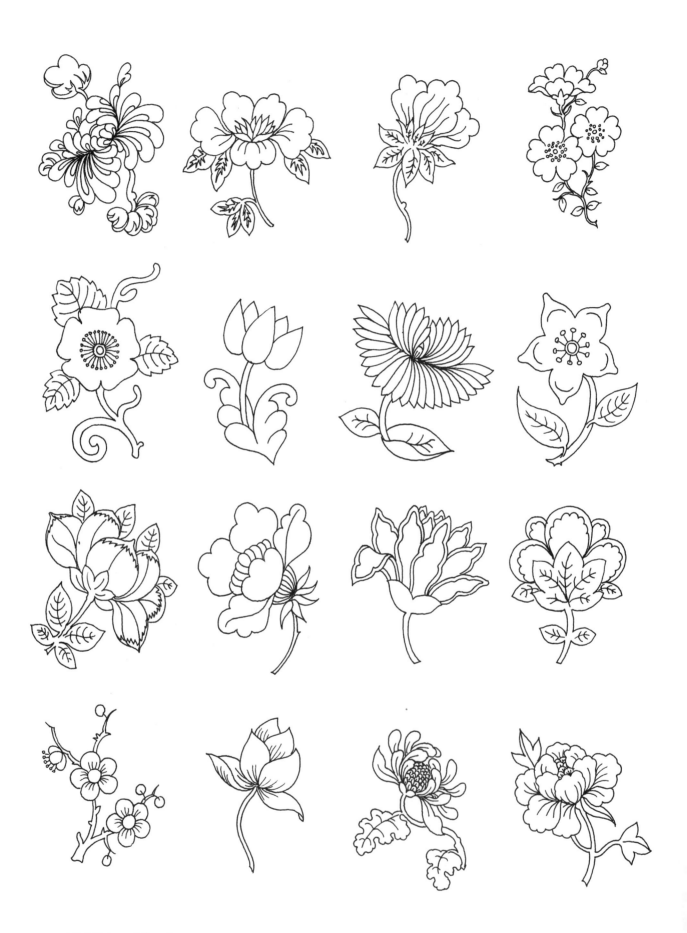

PLATE 16 / Oriental florals

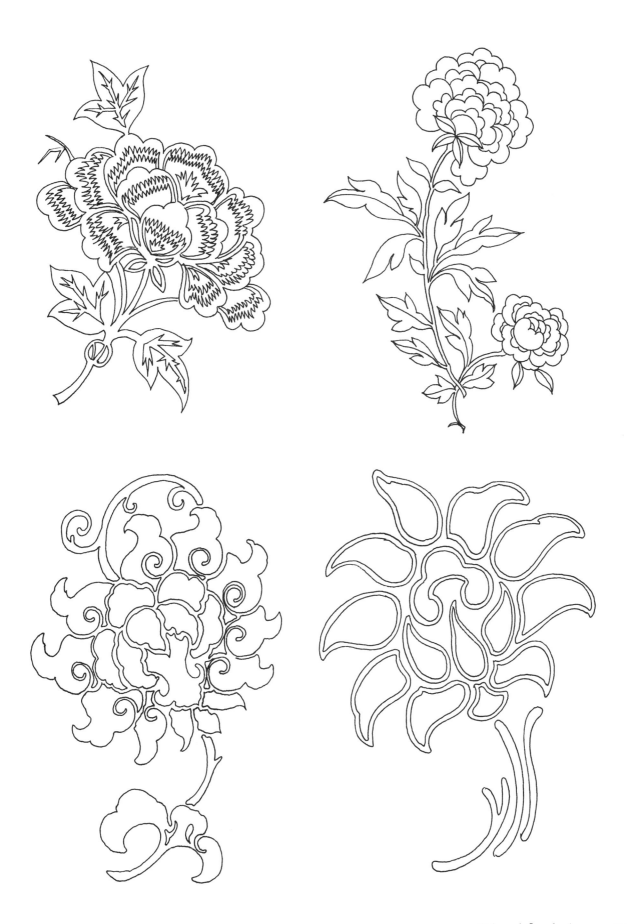

Oriental florals / PLATE 17

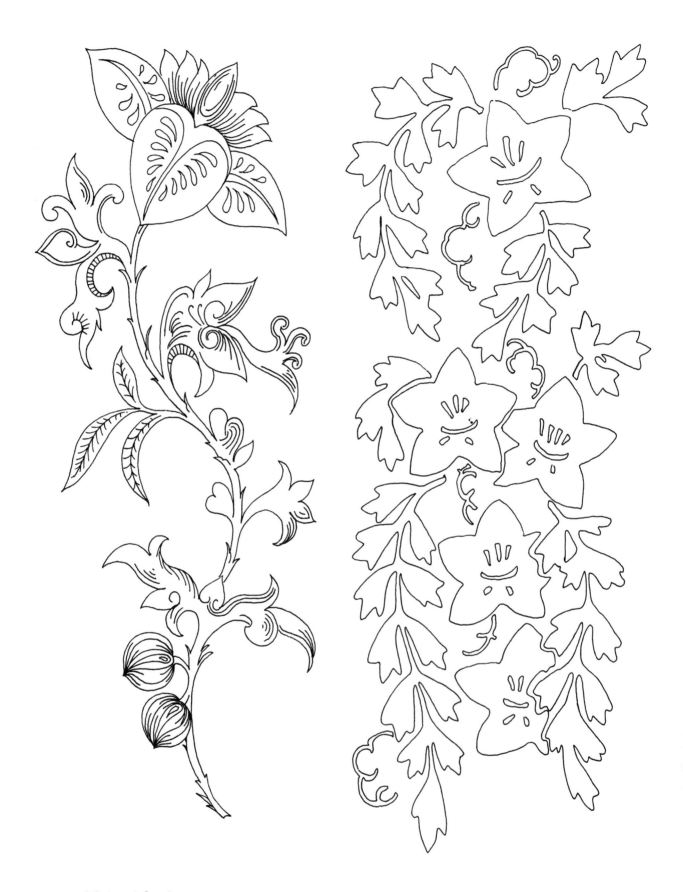

PLATE 18 / Oriental florals

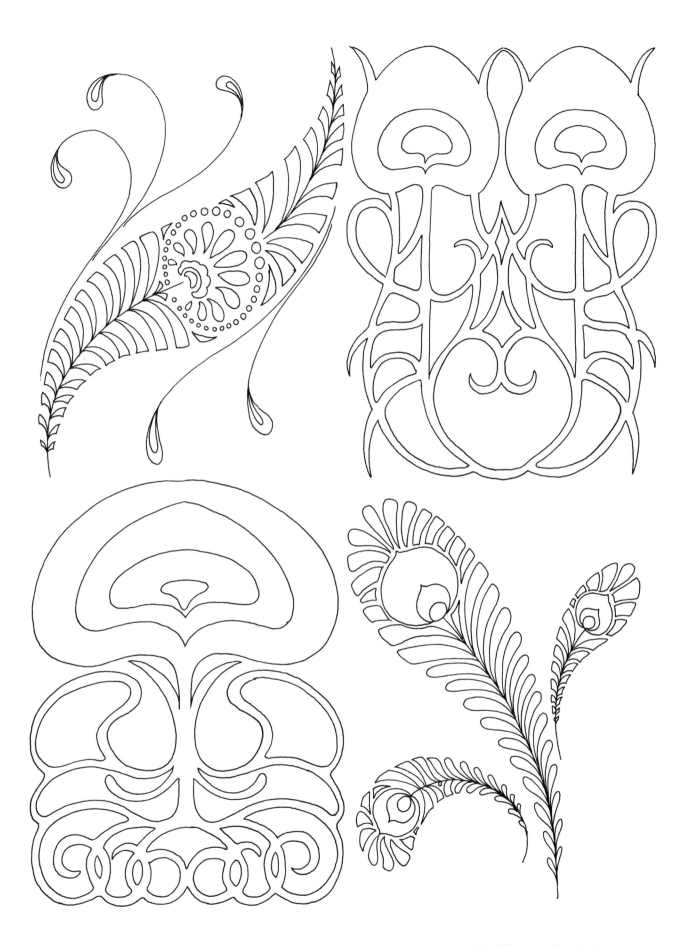

Art Nouveau florals / PLATE 19

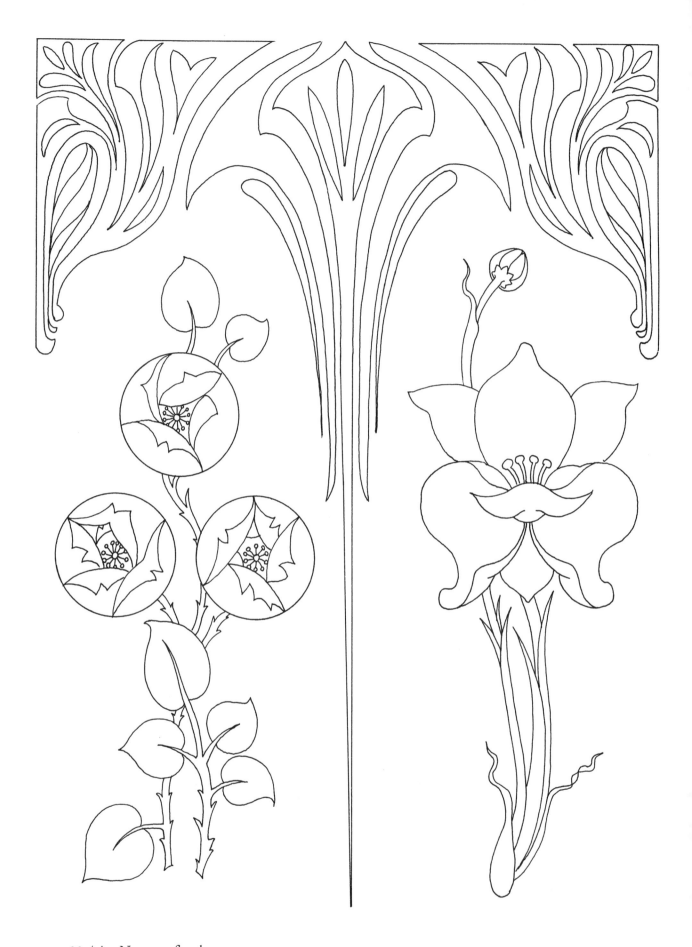

PLATE 20 / Art Nouveau florals

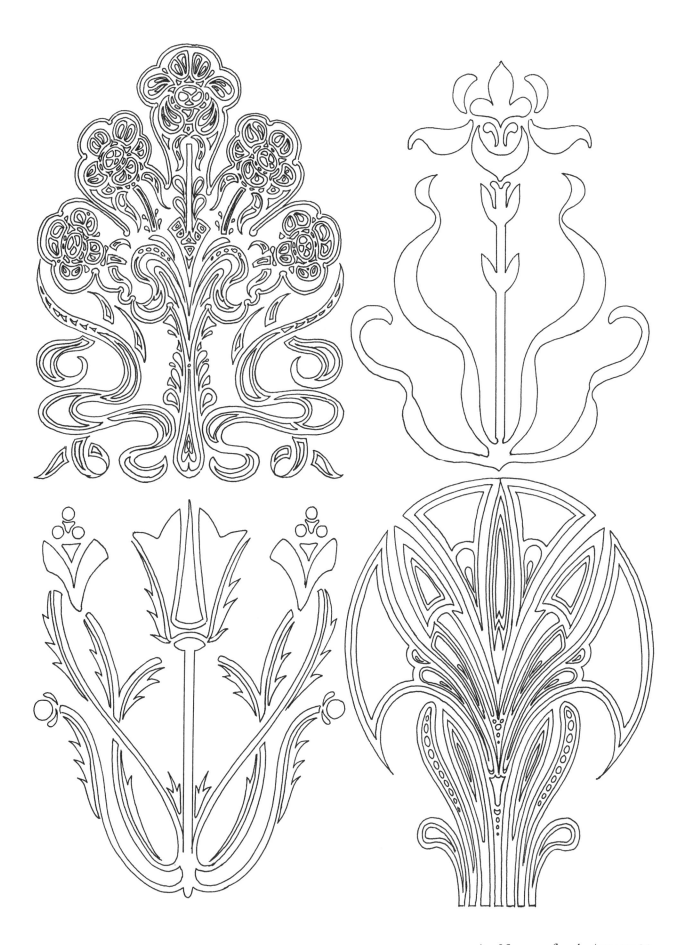

Art Nouveau florals / PLATE 21

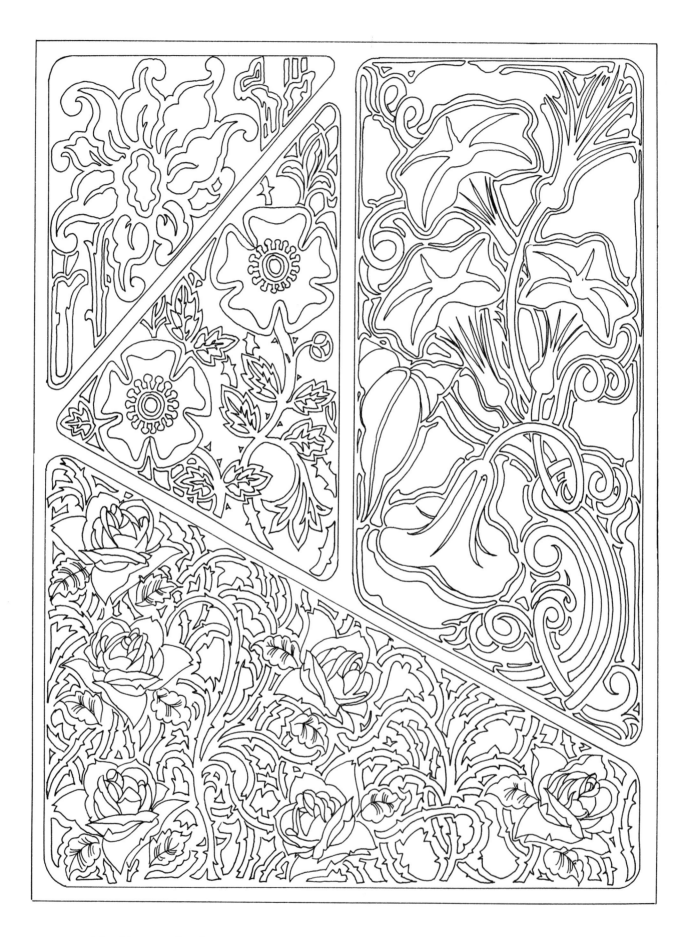

PLATE 22 / Art Nouveau florals

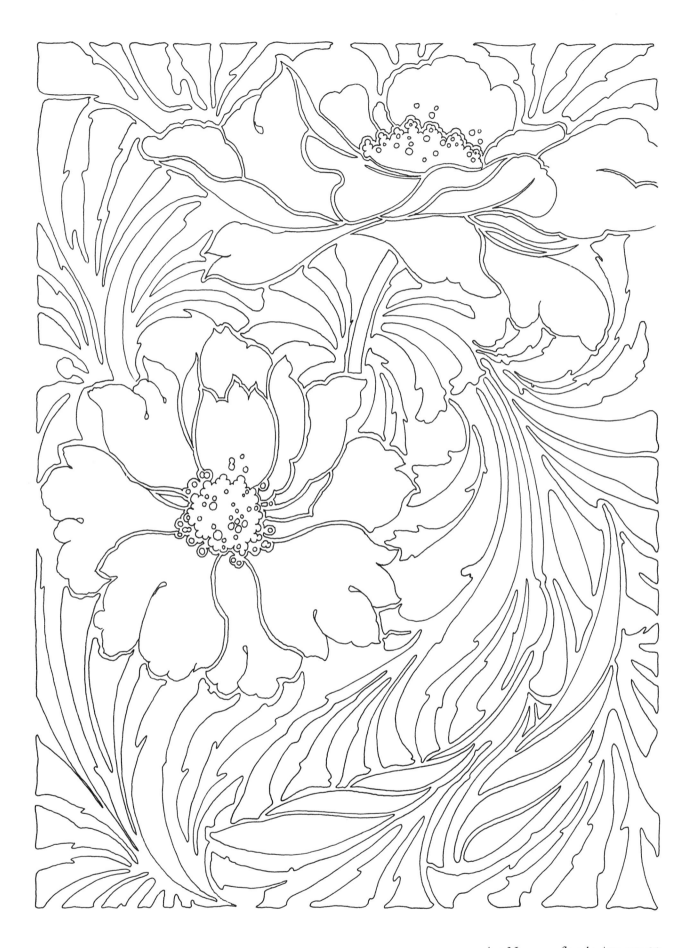

Art Nouveau florals / PLATE 23

Paisleys

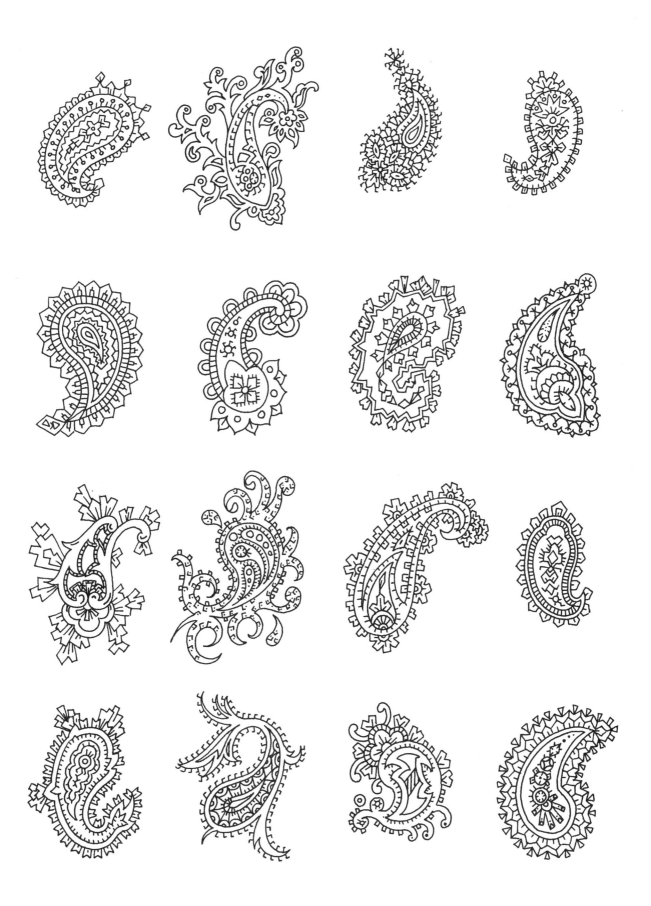

small single paisleys / PLATE 24

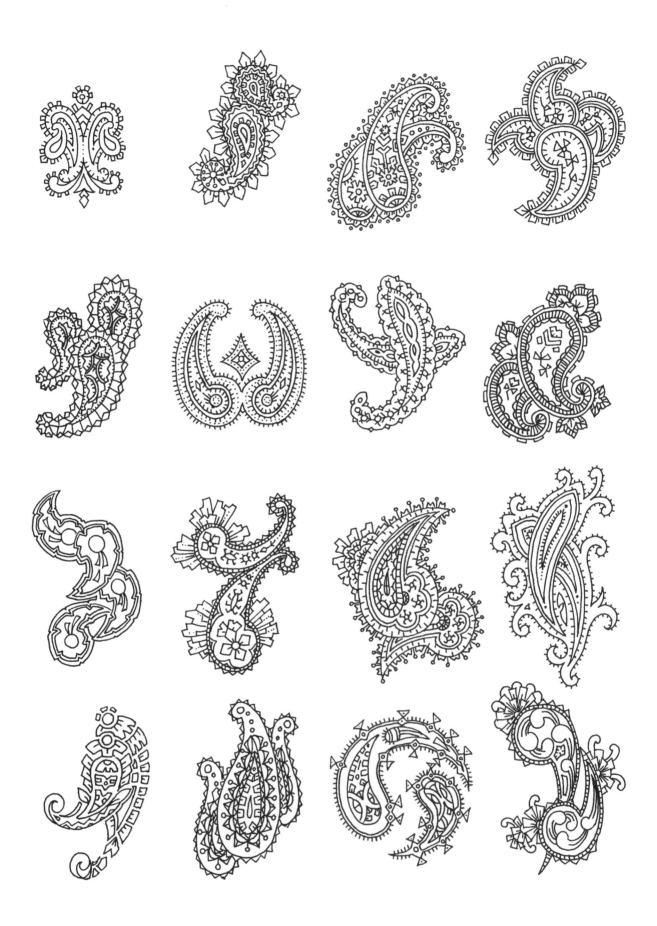

PLATE 25 / small double paisleys

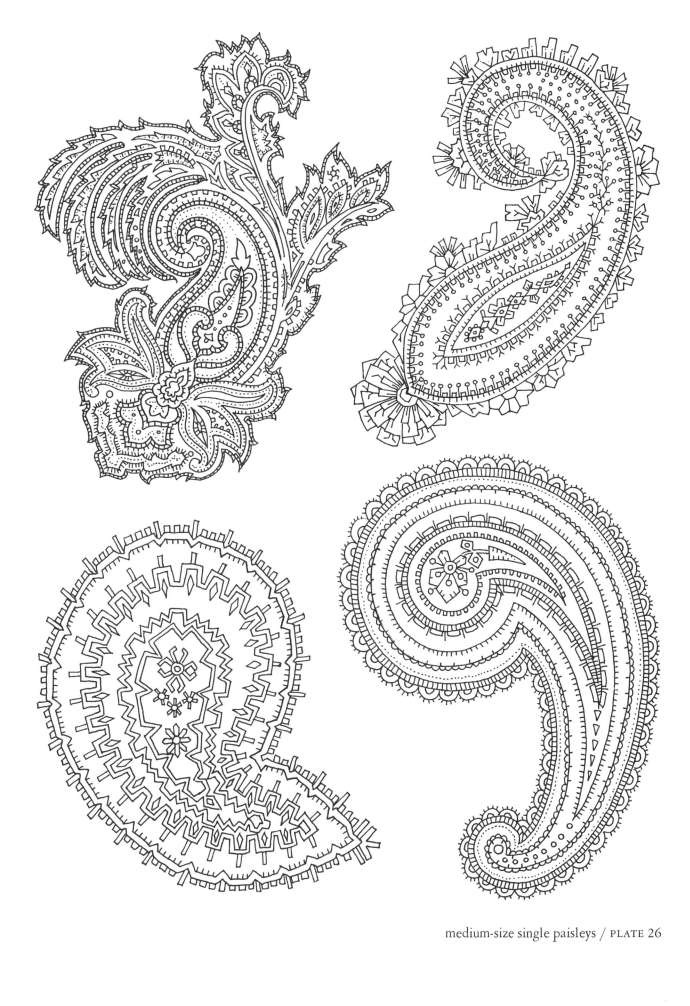

medium-size single paisleys / PLATE 26

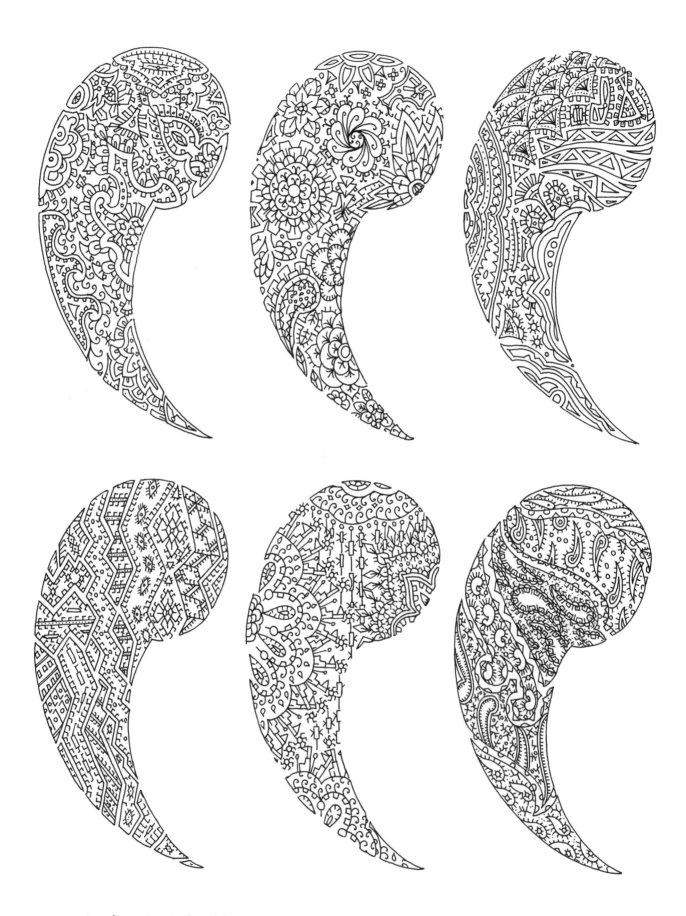

PLATE 27 / medium-size single paisleys

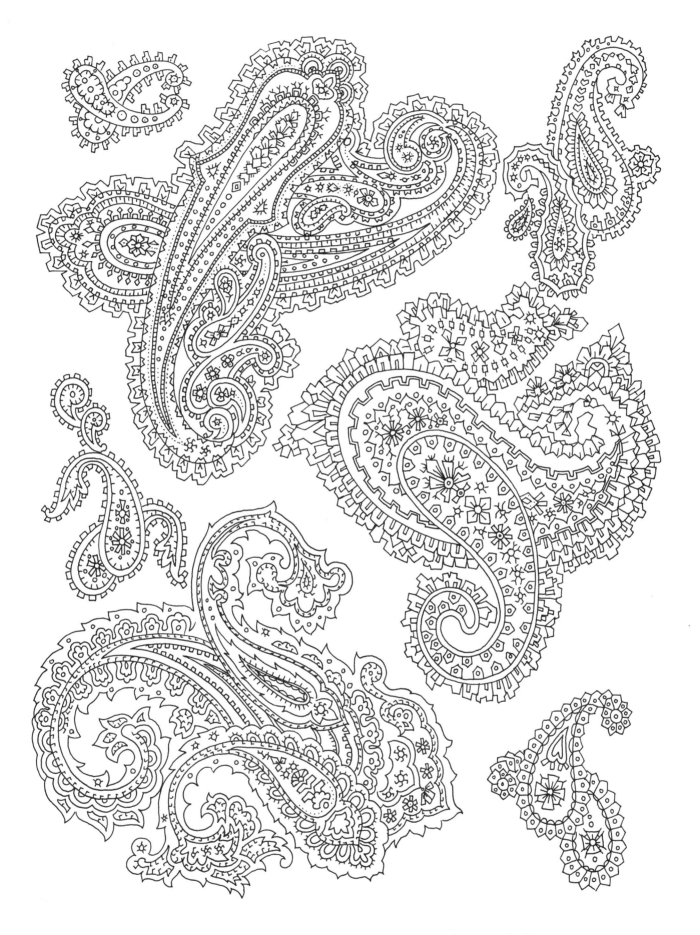

medium-size double paisleys / PLATE 28

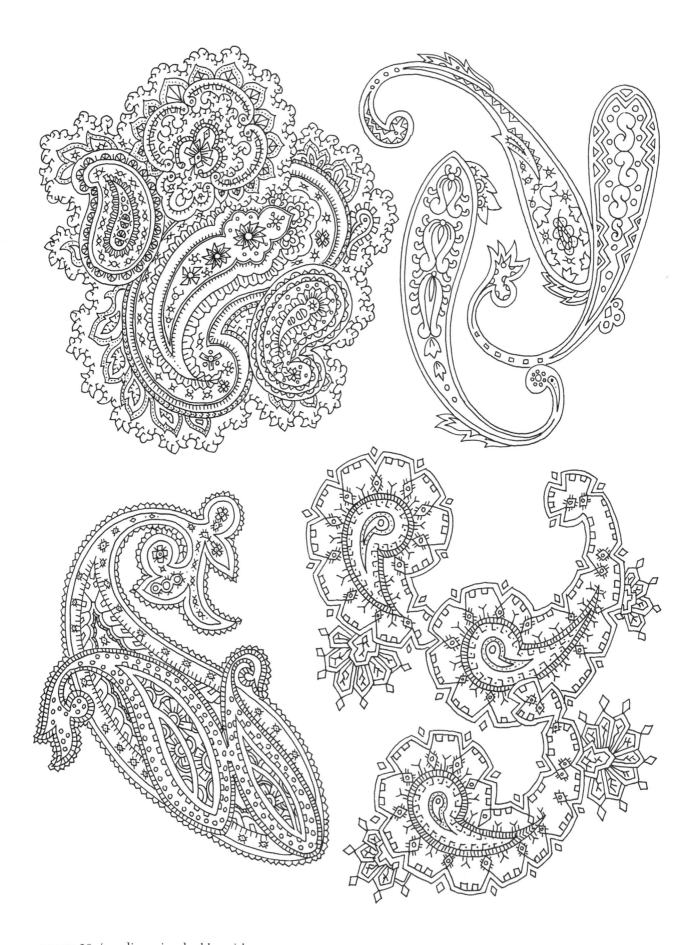

PLATE 29 / medium-size double paisleys

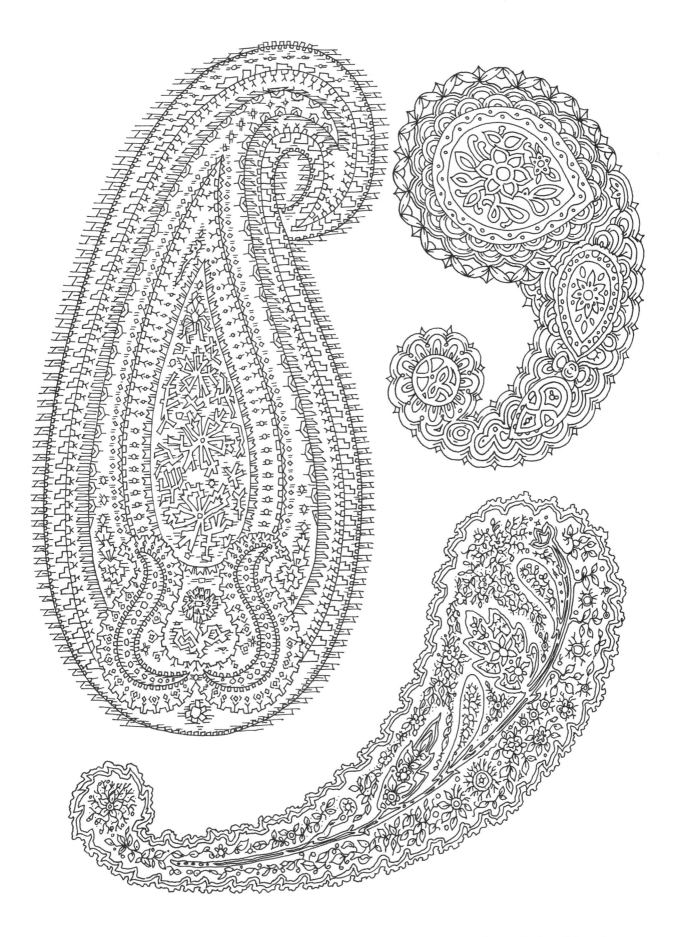

large single paisleys / PLATE 30

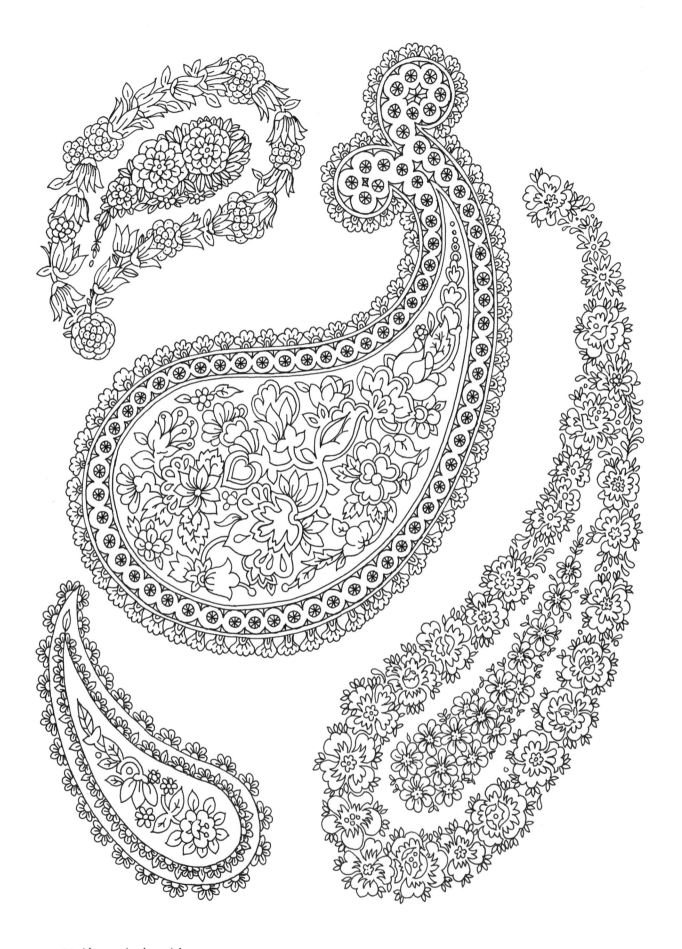

PLATE 31 / large single paisleys

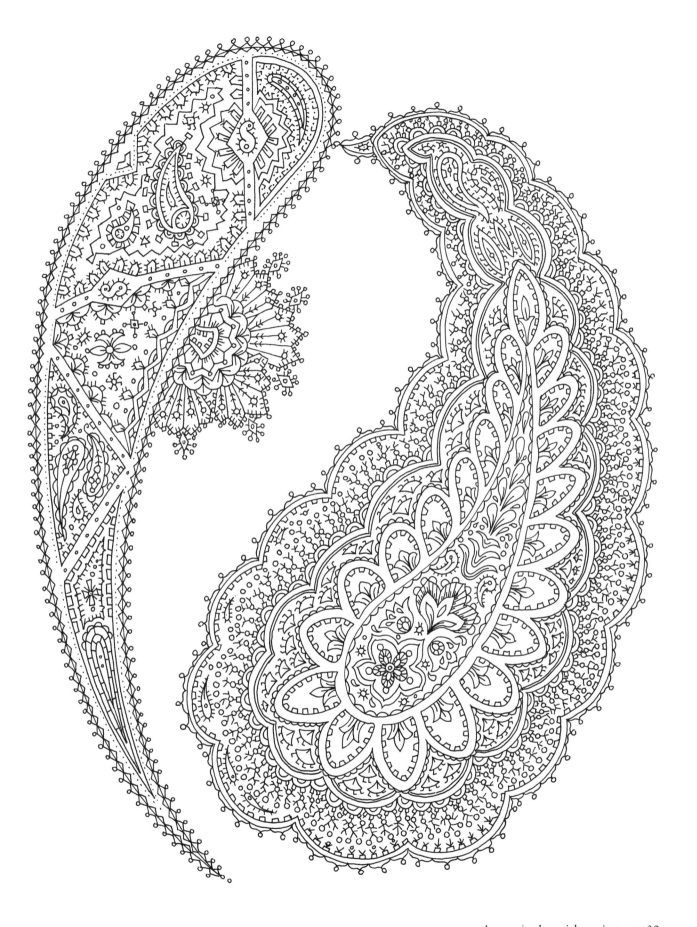

large single paisleys / PLATE 32

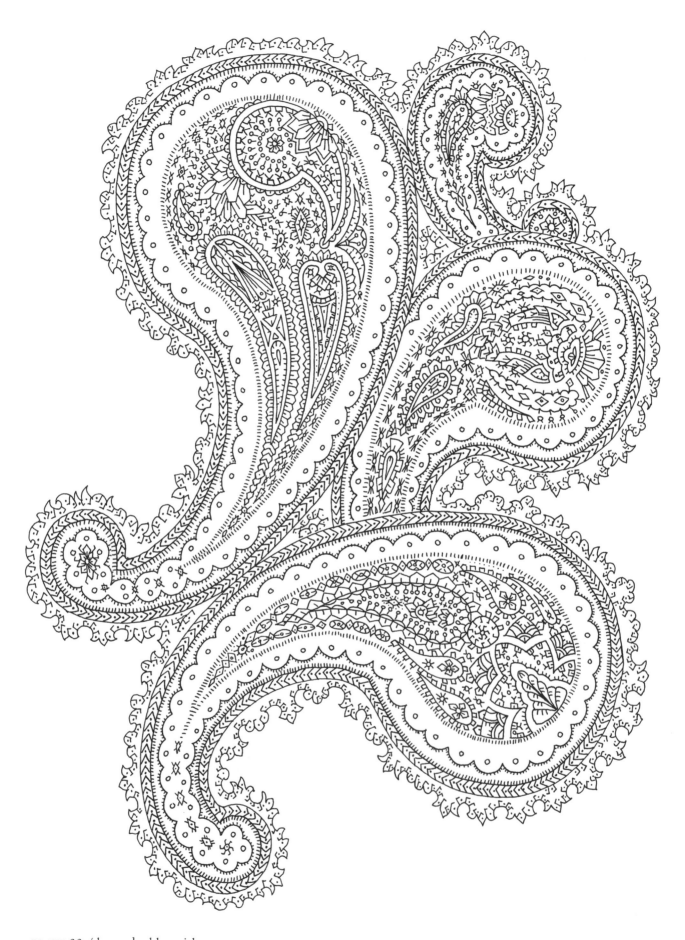

PLATE 33 / large double paisleys

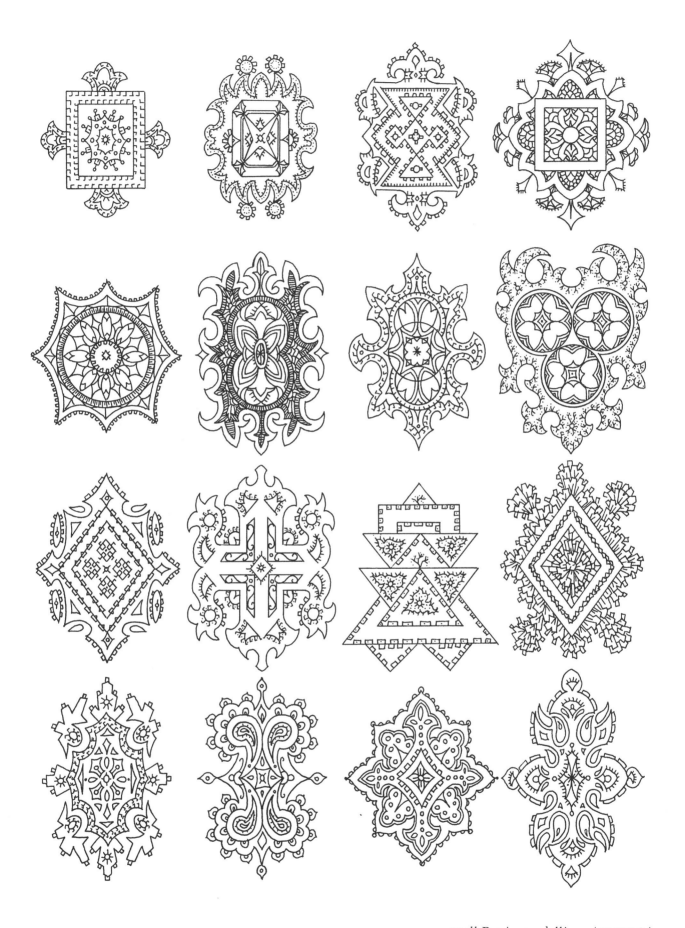

small Persian medallions / PLATE 34

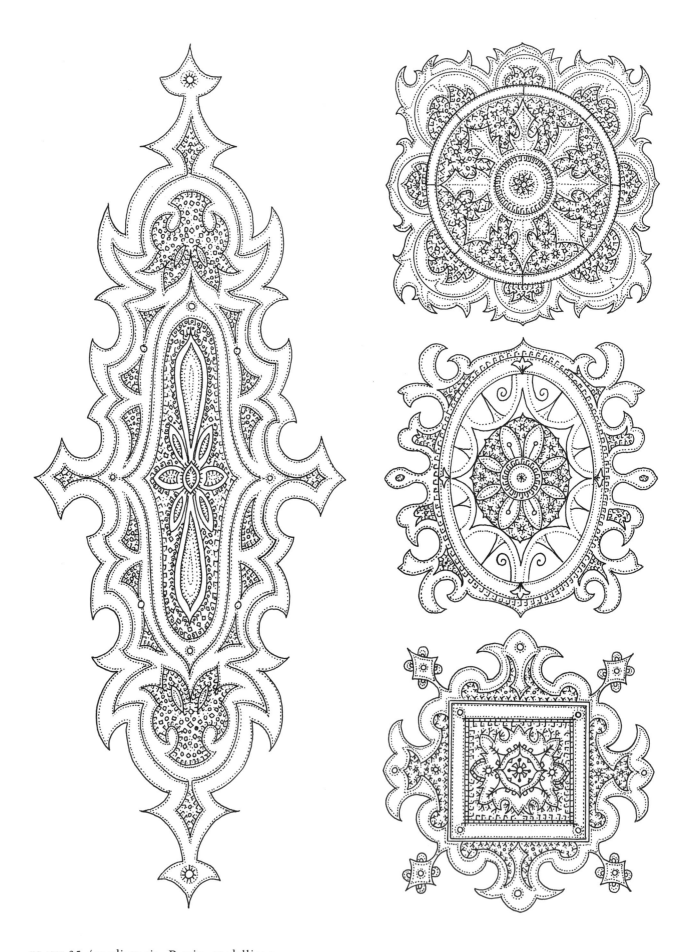

PLATE 35 / medium-size Persian medallions

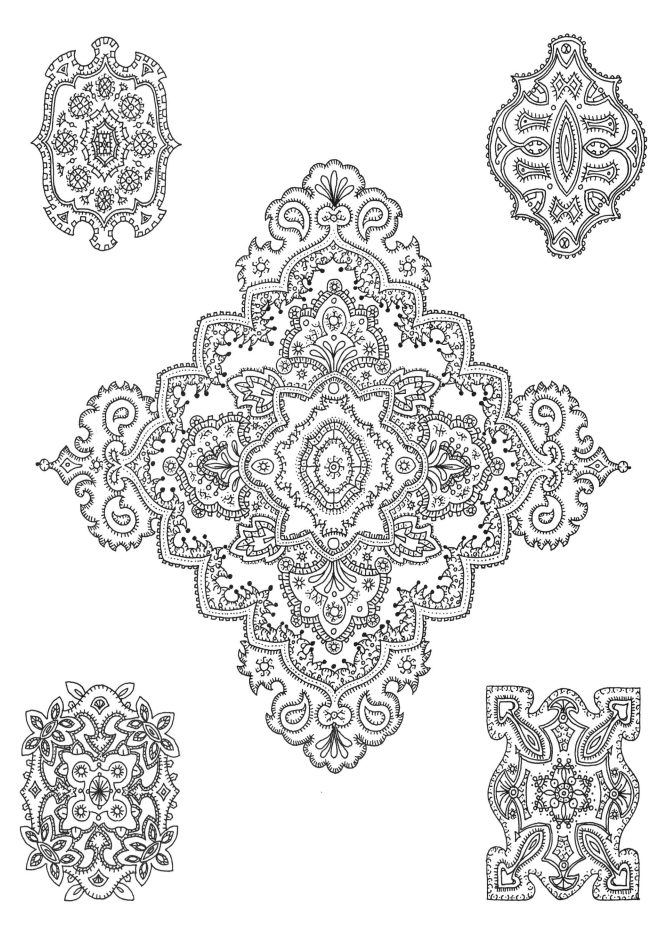

medium-size Persian medallions / PLATE 36

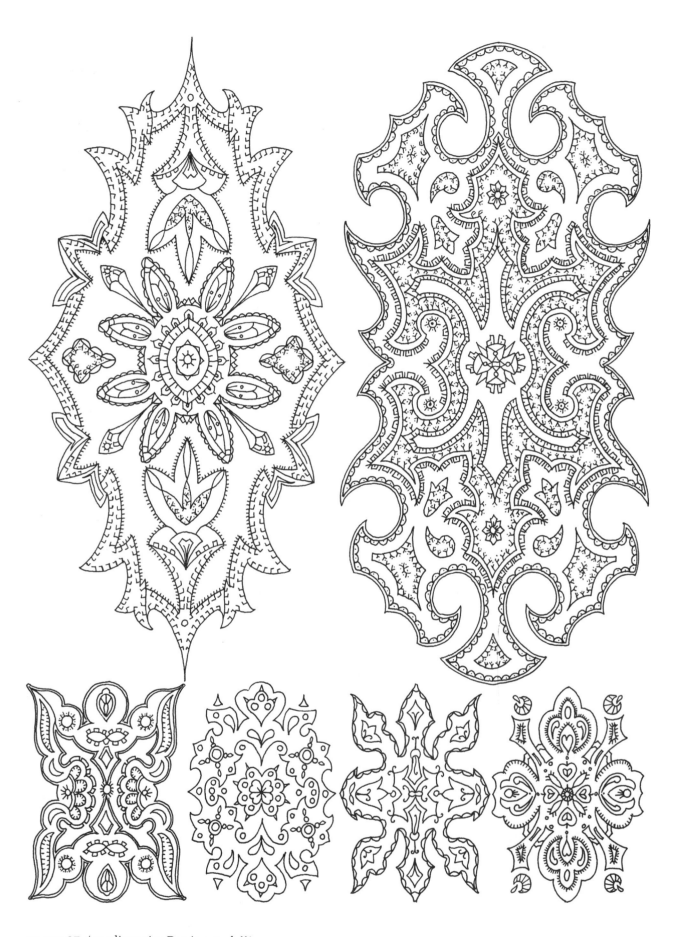

PLATE 37 / medium-size Persian medallions

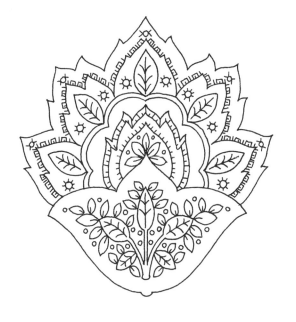
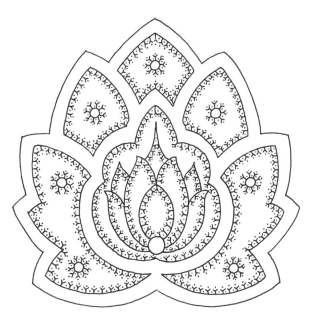
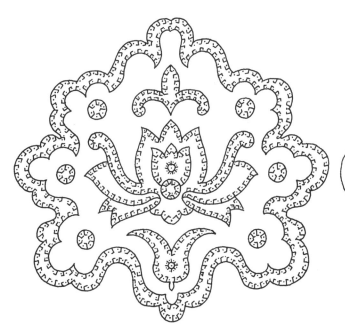
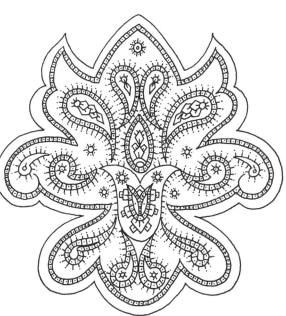

medium-size Persian medallions / PLATE 38

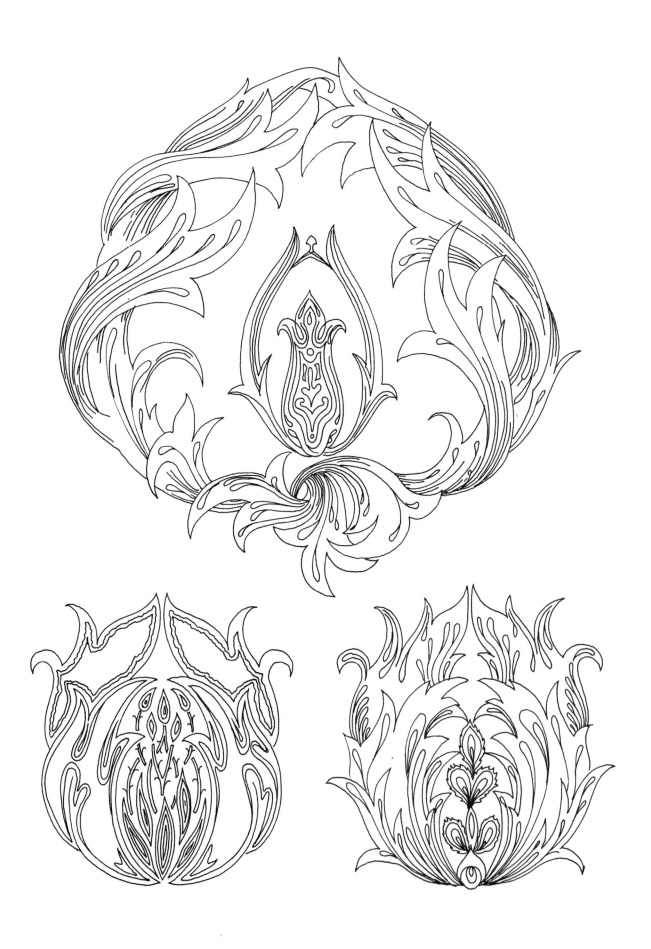

PLATE 39 / Art Nouveau medallions

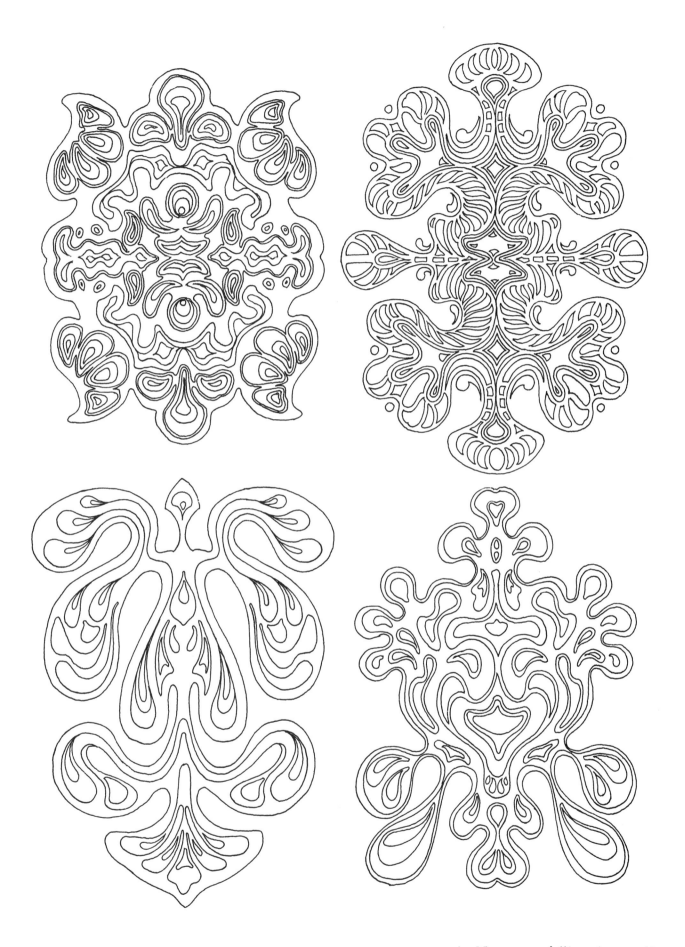

Art Nouveau medallions / PLATE 40

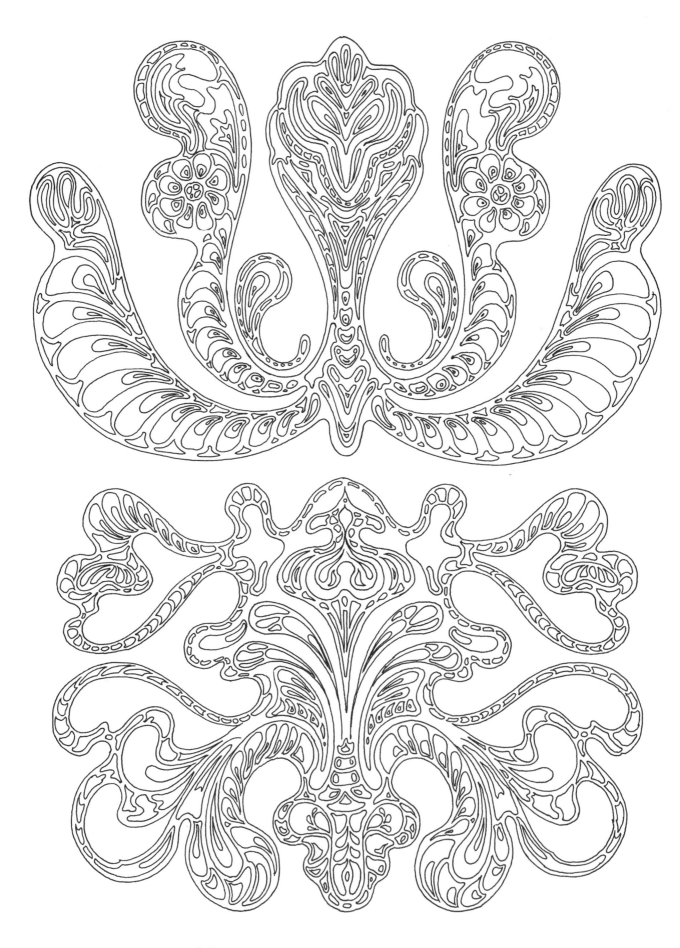

PLATE 41 / Art Nouveau medallions

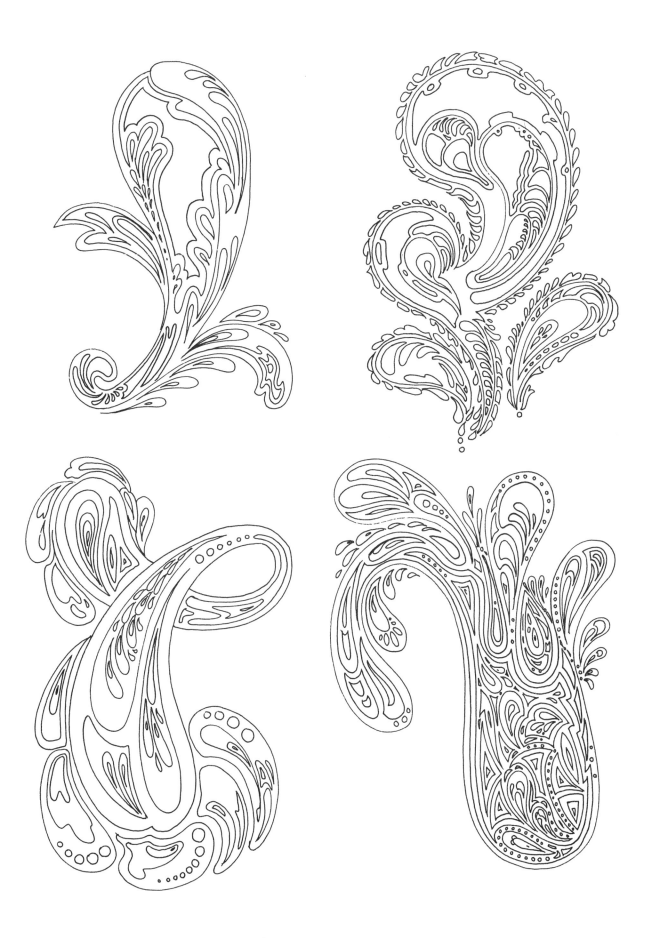

Art Nouveau paisleys / PLATE 42

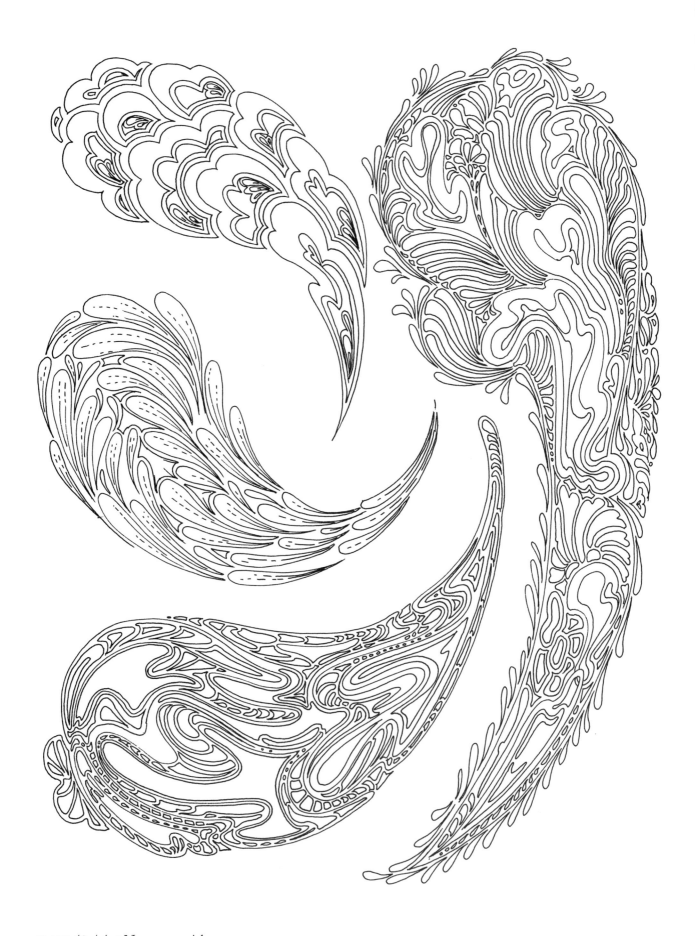

PLATE 43 / Art Nouveau paisleys

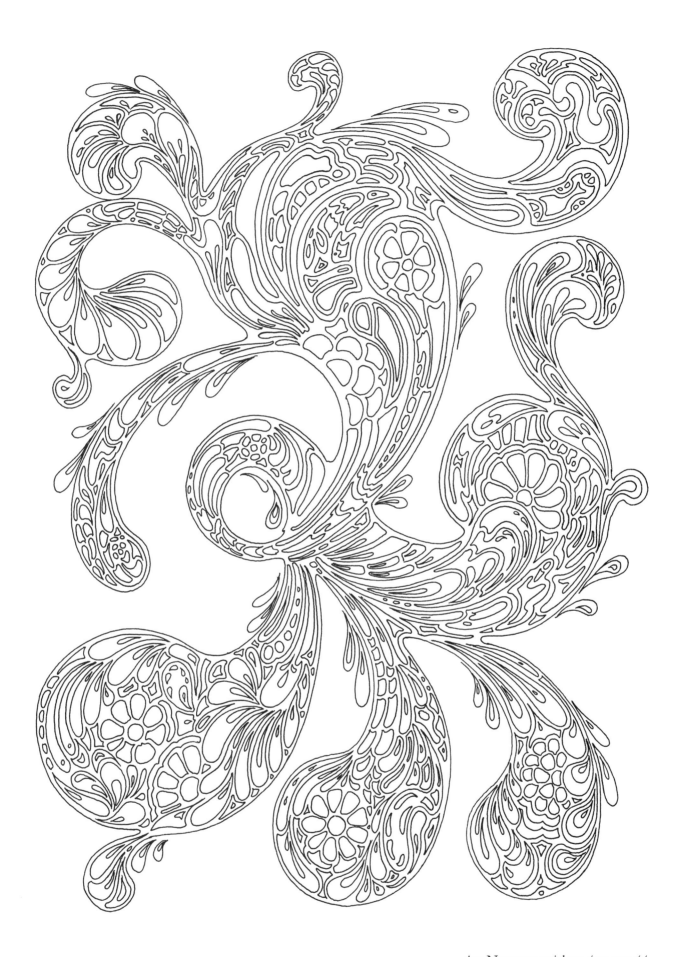

Art Nouveau paisleys / PLATE 44

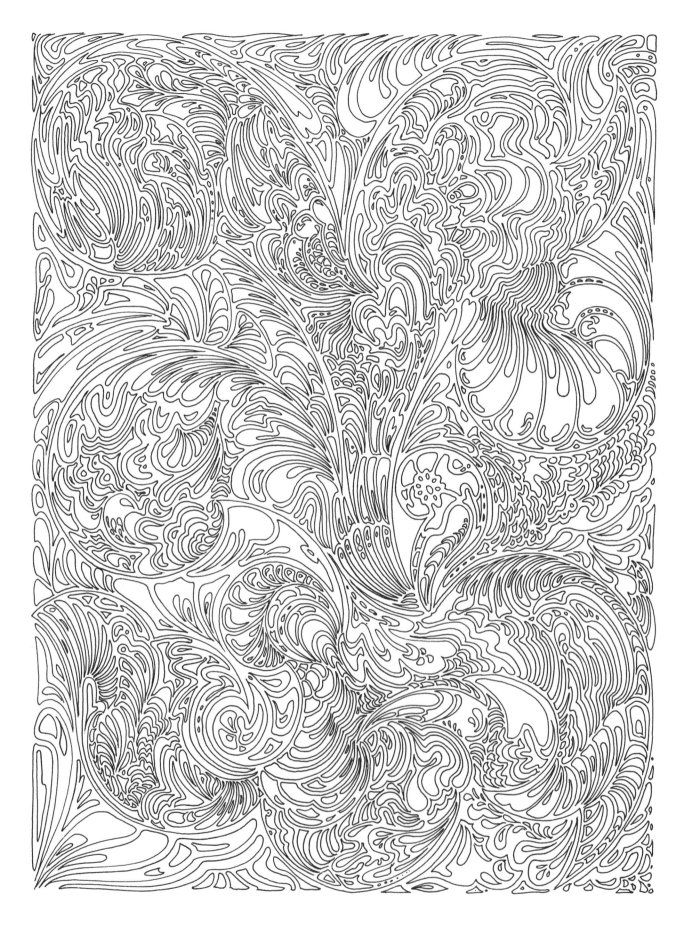

PLATE 45 / Art Nouveau paisleys

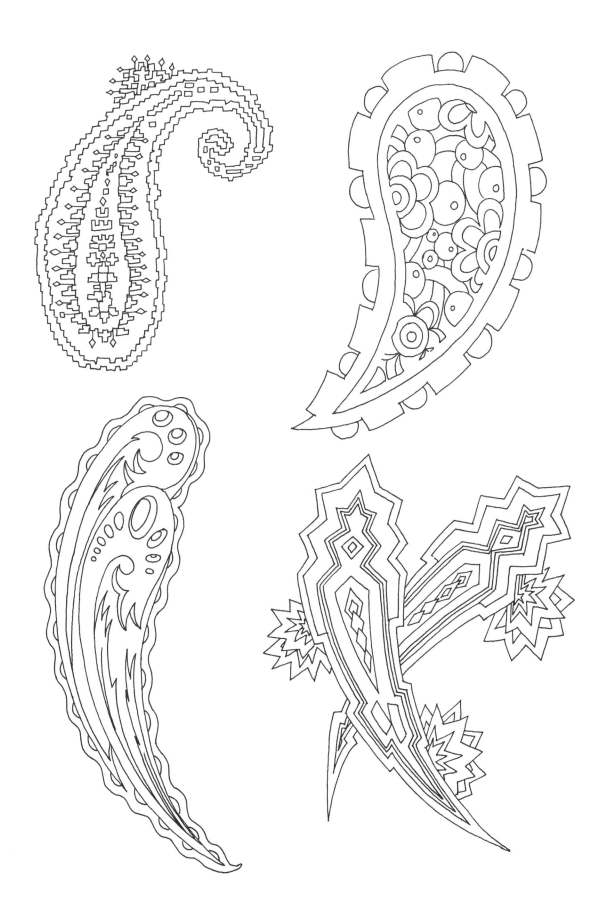

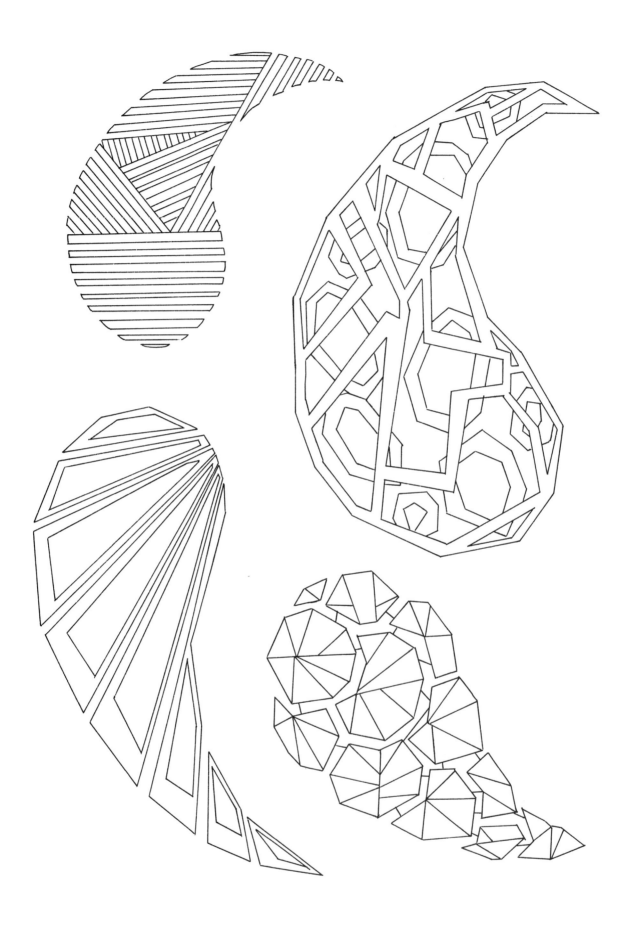

PLATE 47 / modern paisleys

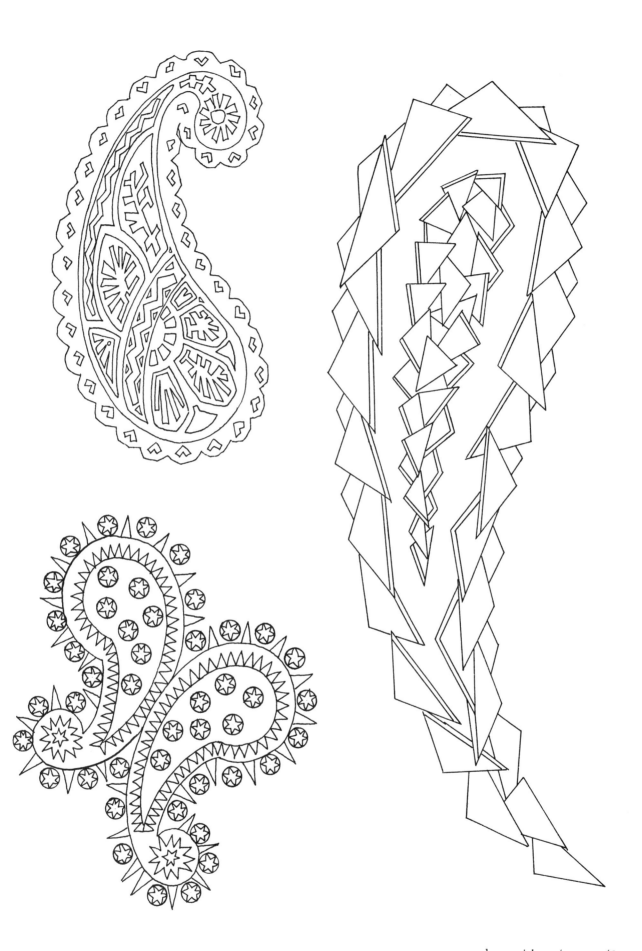

modern paisleys / PLATE 48

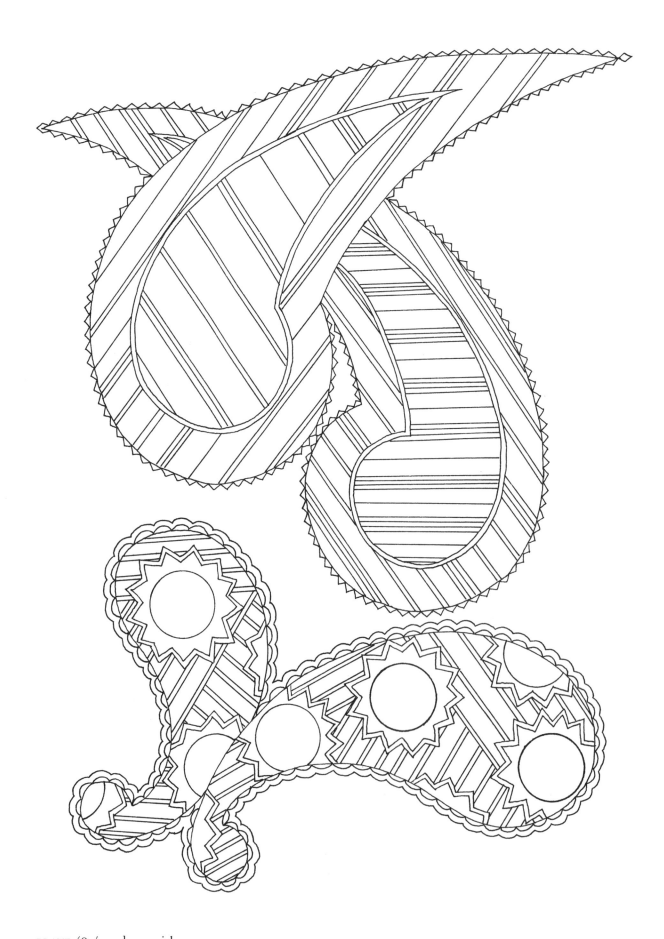

PLATE 49 / modern paisleys

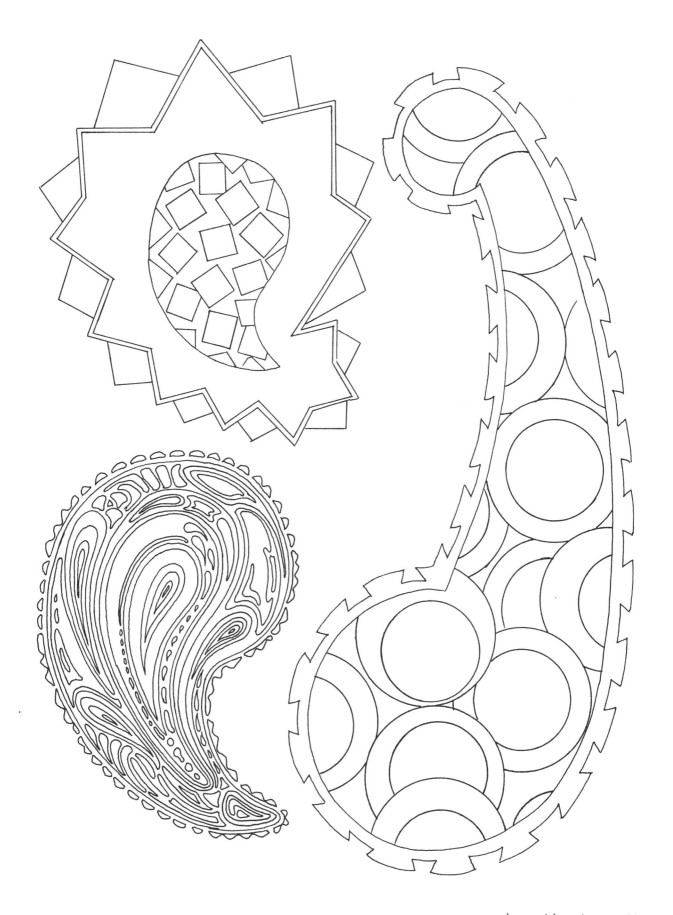

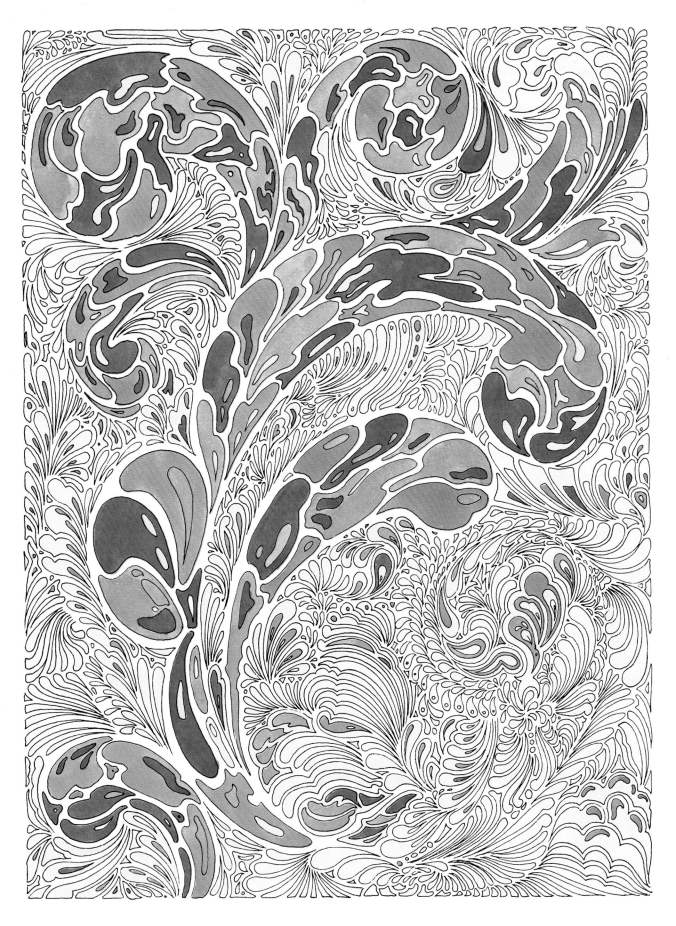

a psychedelic design executed in four colors / PLATE A

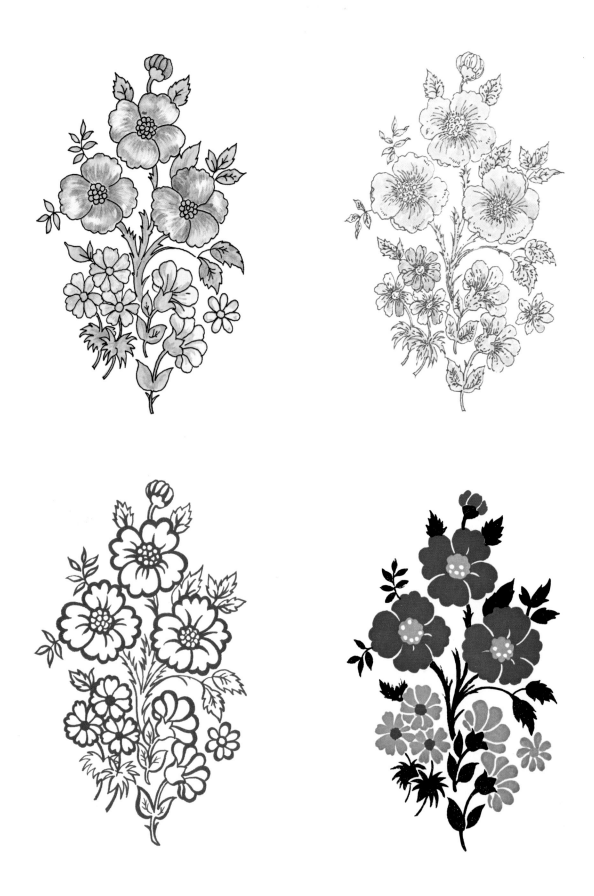

PLATE B / the same motif rendered four different ways

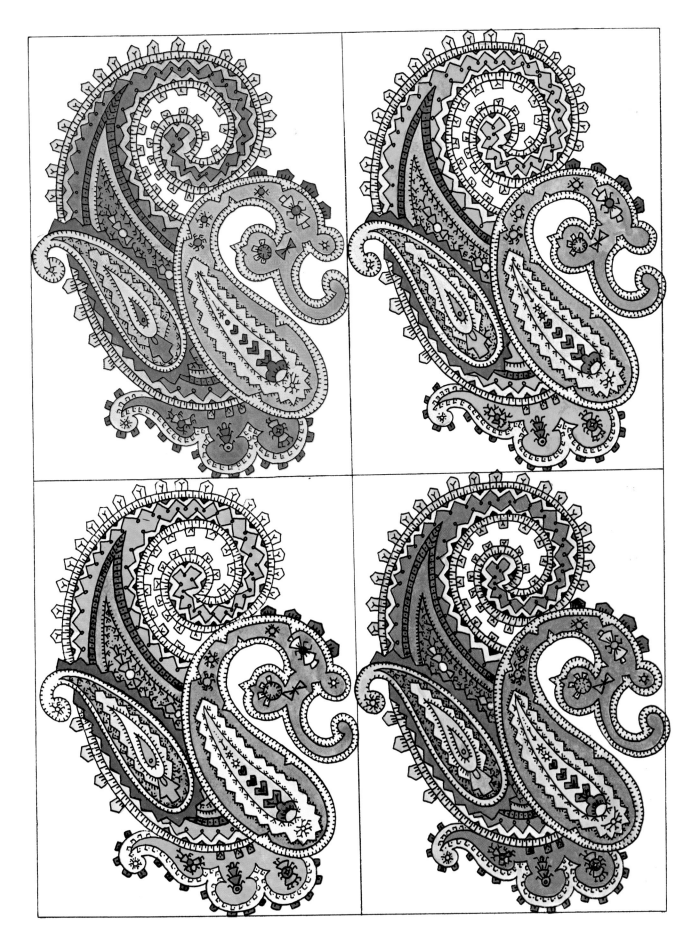

four different color treatments of the same motif / PLATE C

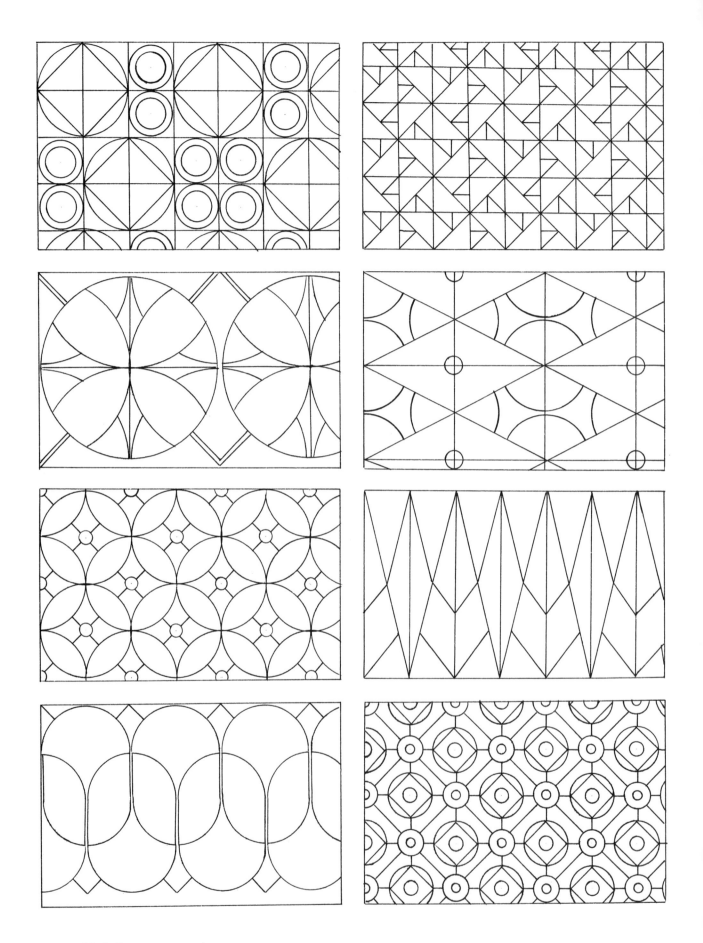

PLATE 52 / all-over geometrics

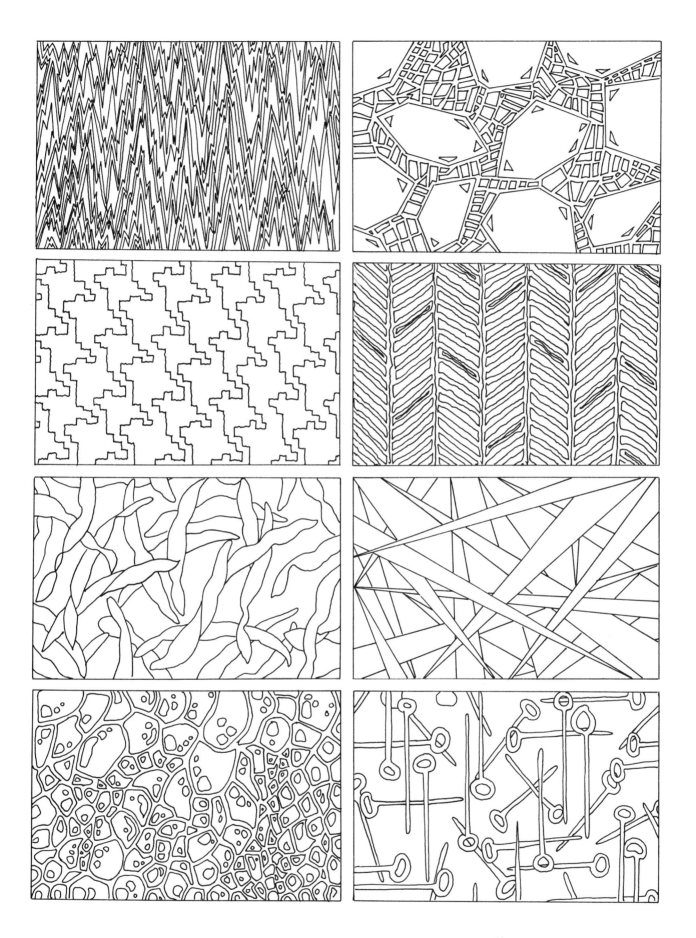

all-over geometrics / PLATE 53

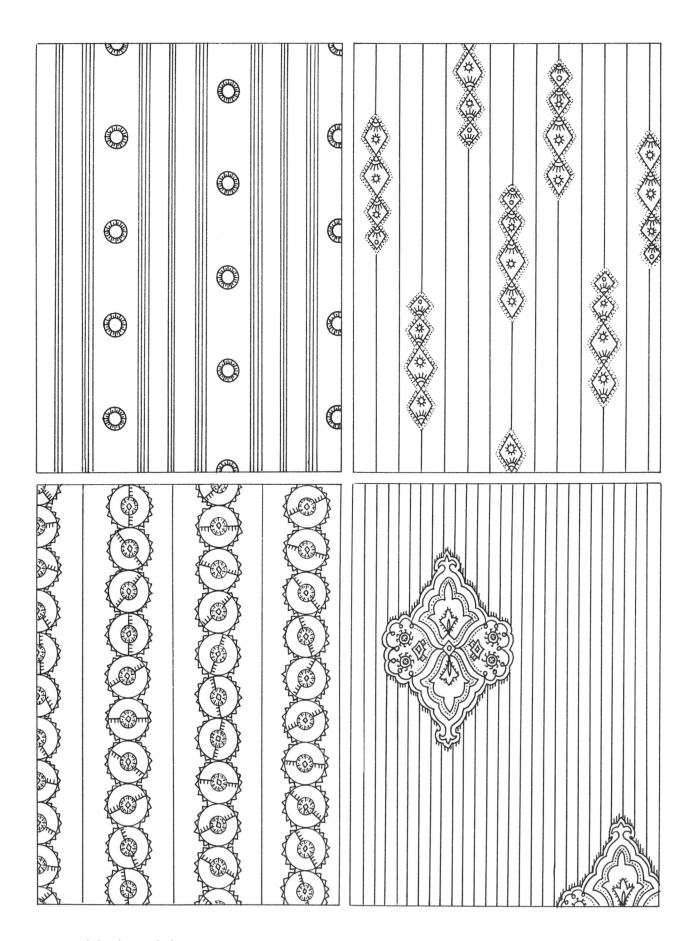

PLATE 54 / stripe variations

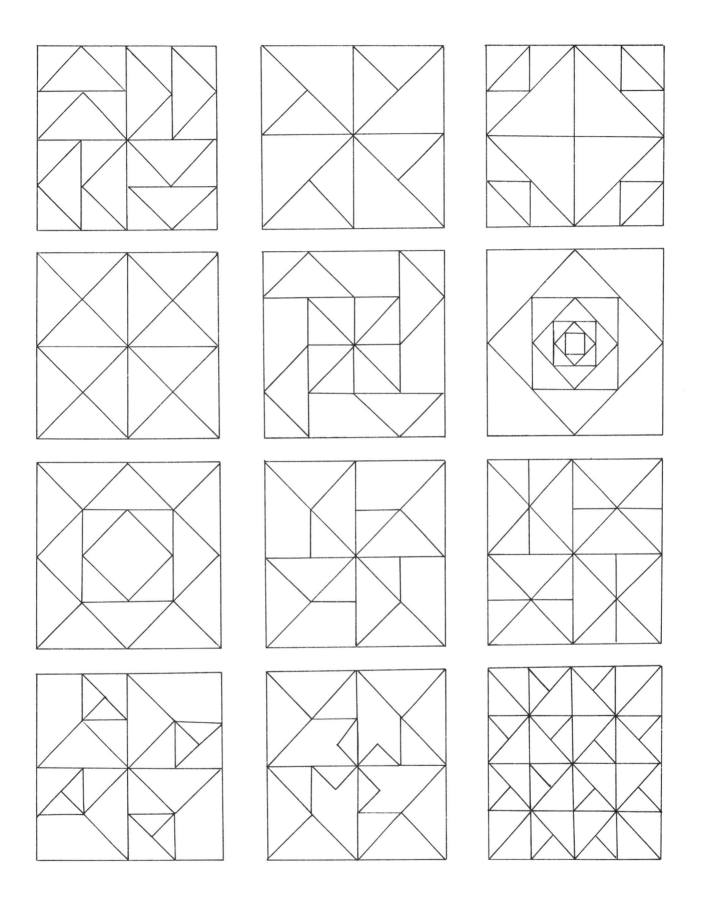

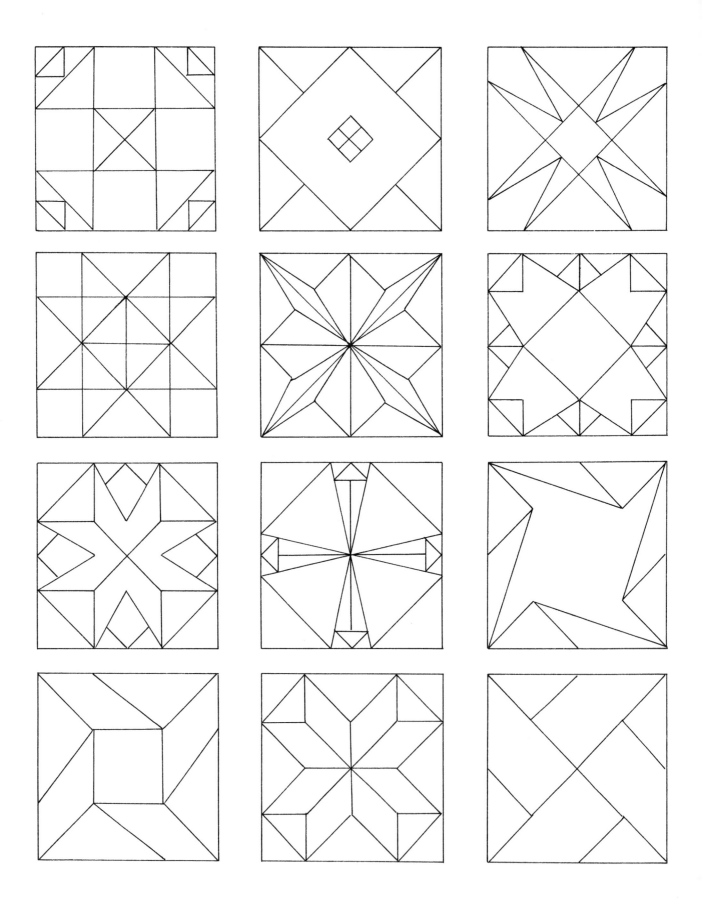

PLATE 56 / quilt geometrics

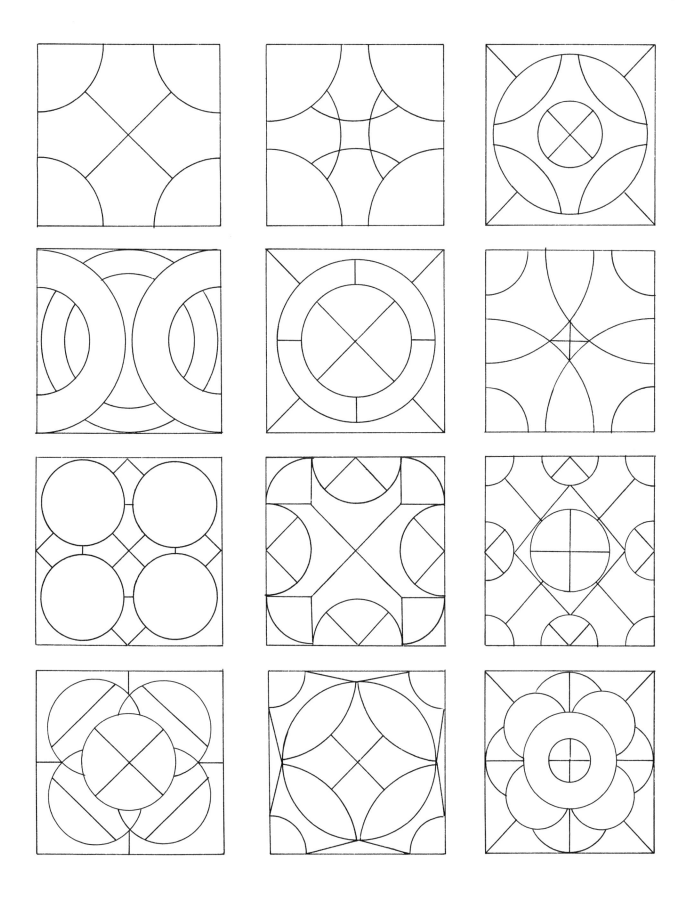

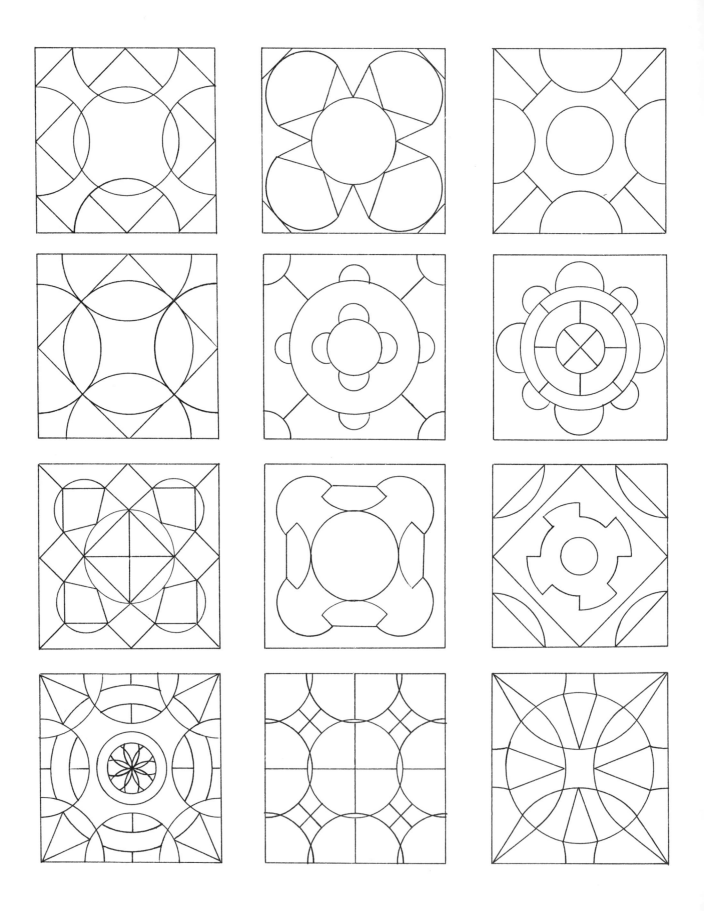

PLATE 58 / quilt geometrics

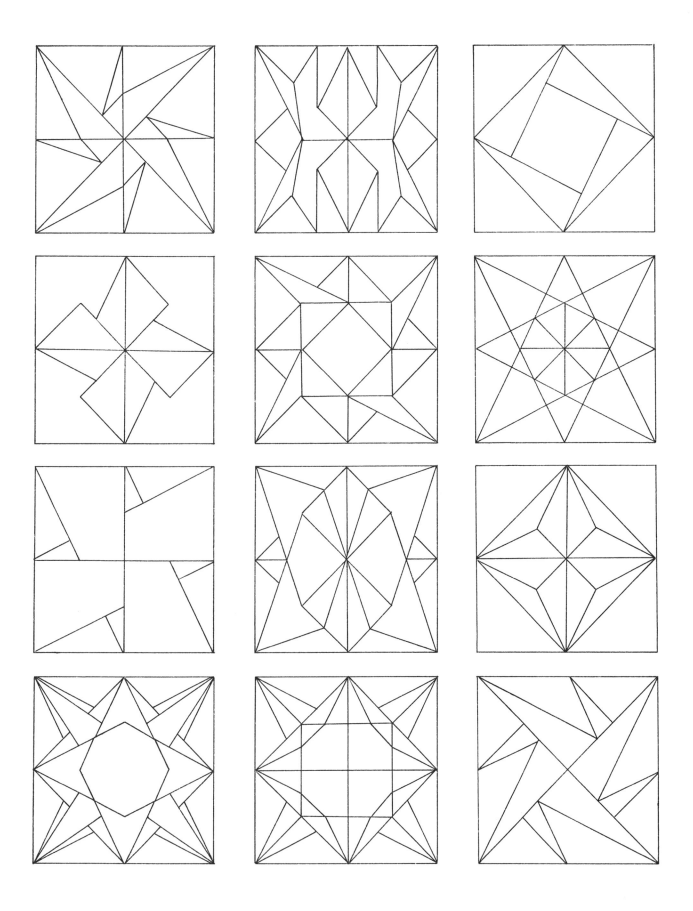

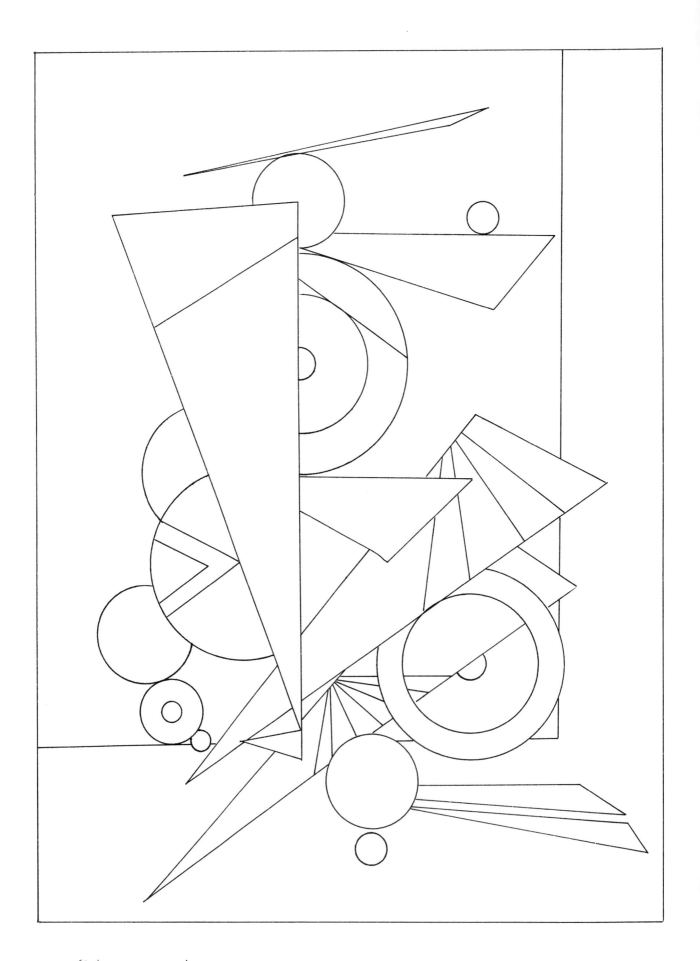

PLATE 60 / op art geometrics

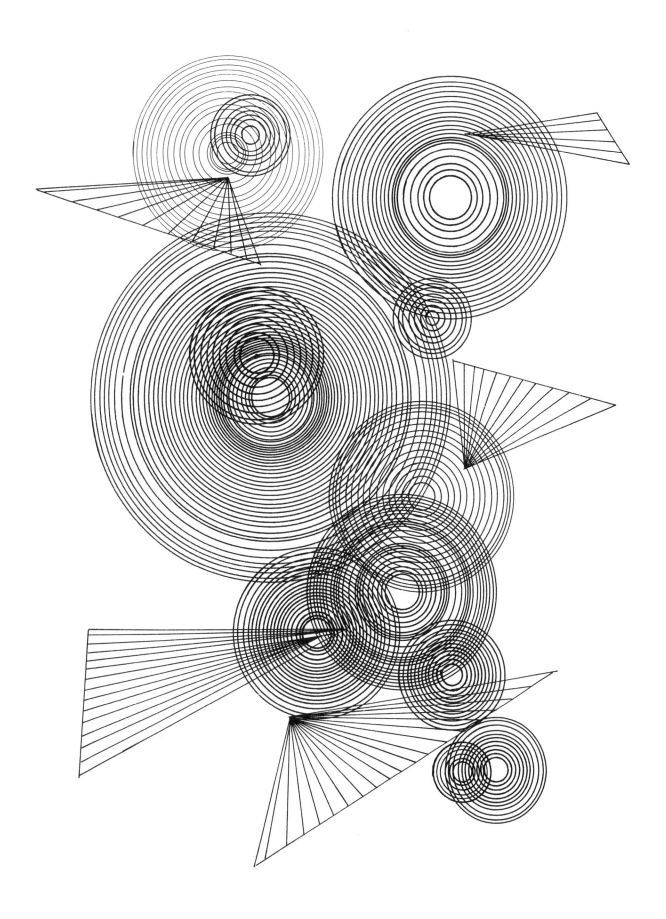

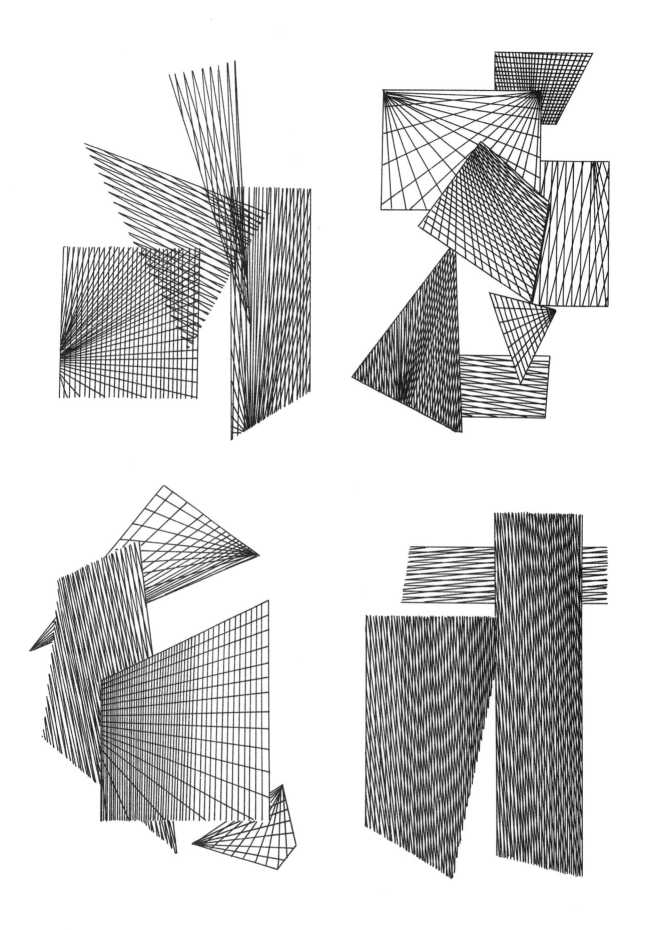

PLATE 62 / op art geometrics

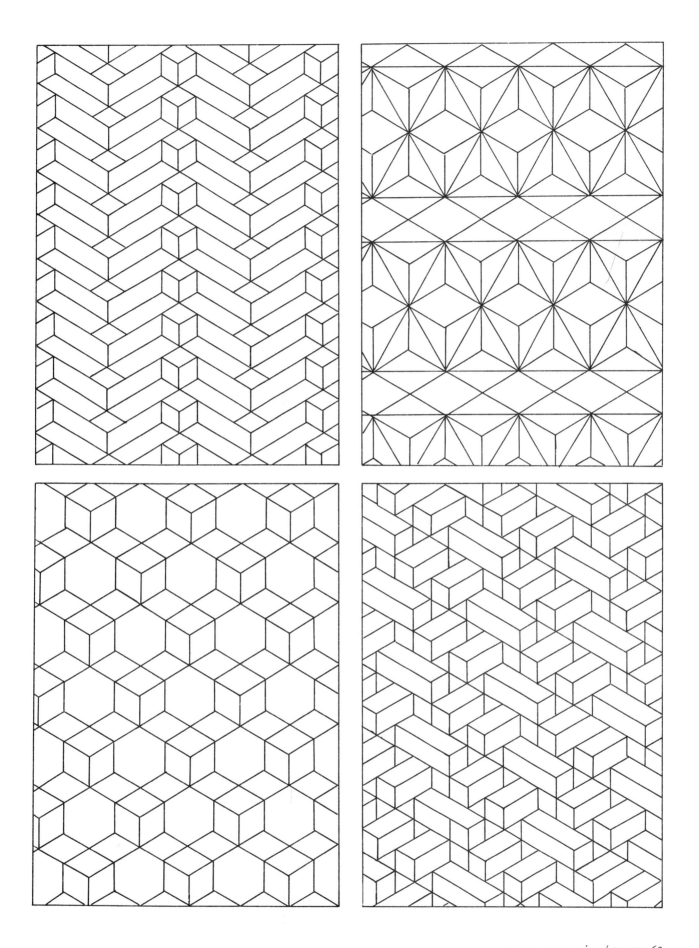

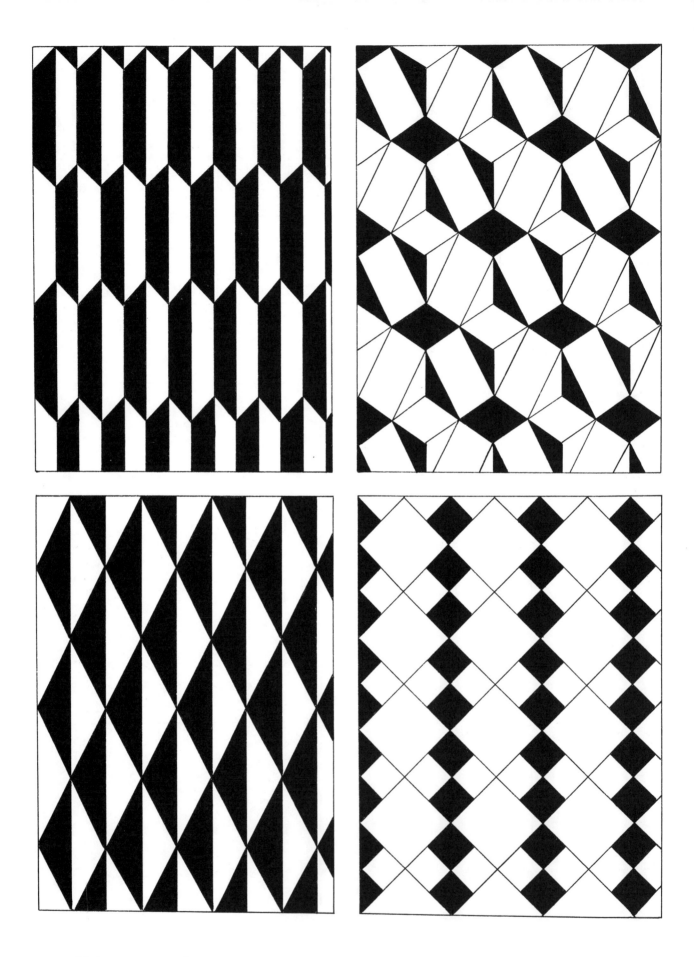

PLATE 64 / op art geometrics

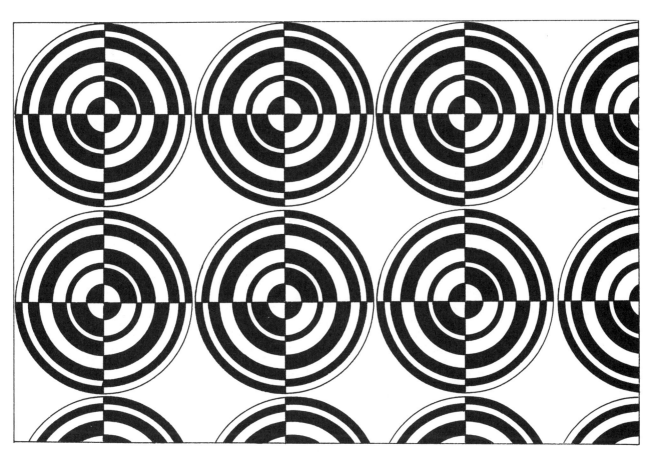

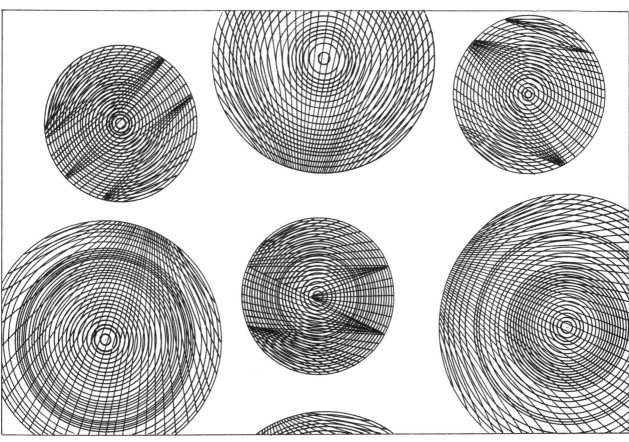

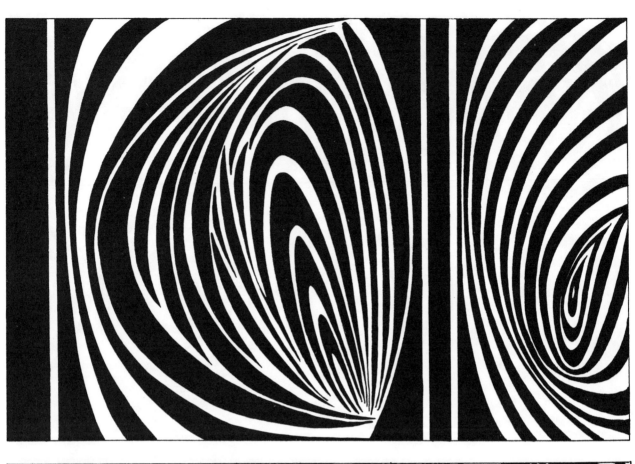

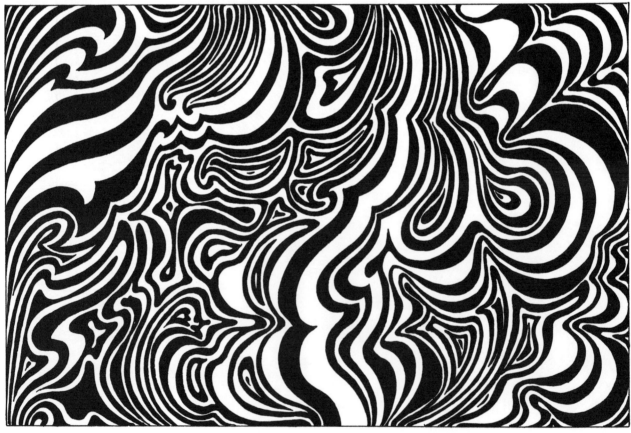

PLATE 66 / op art geometrics

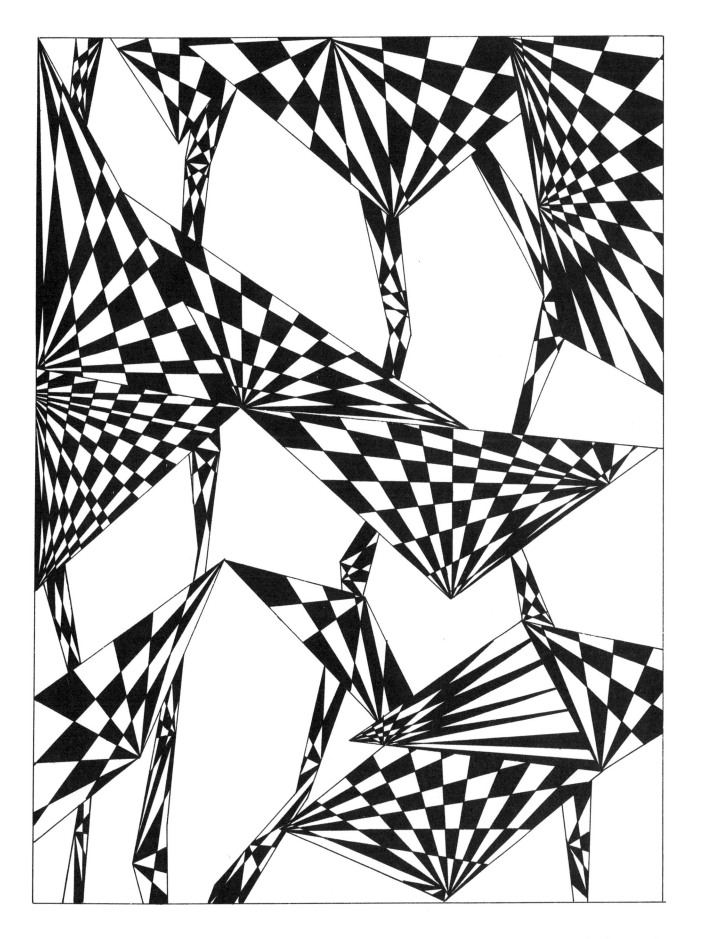

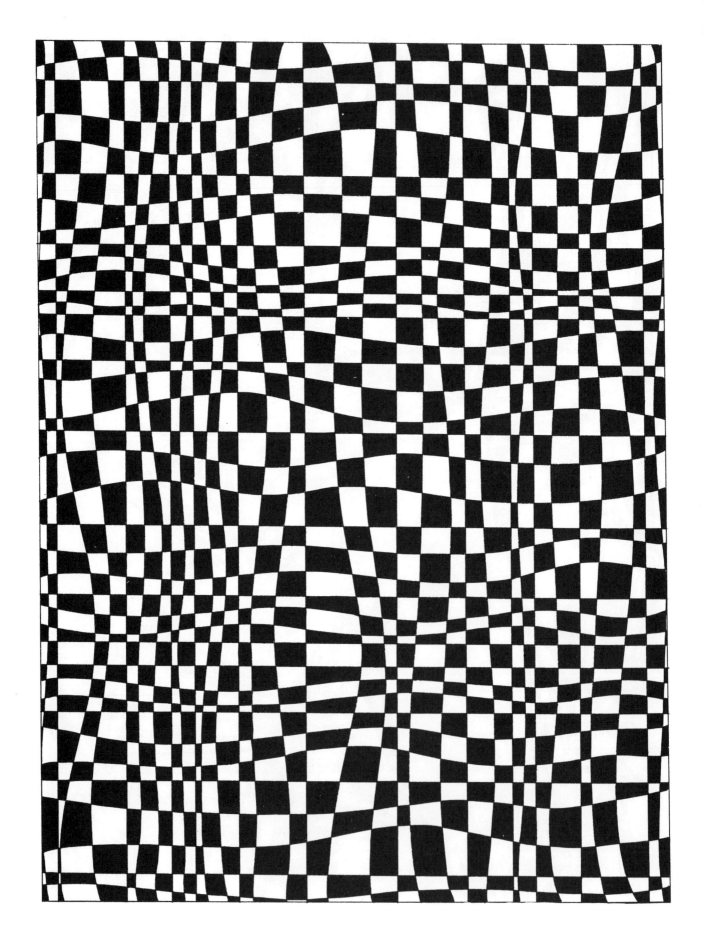

PLATE 68 / op art geometrics

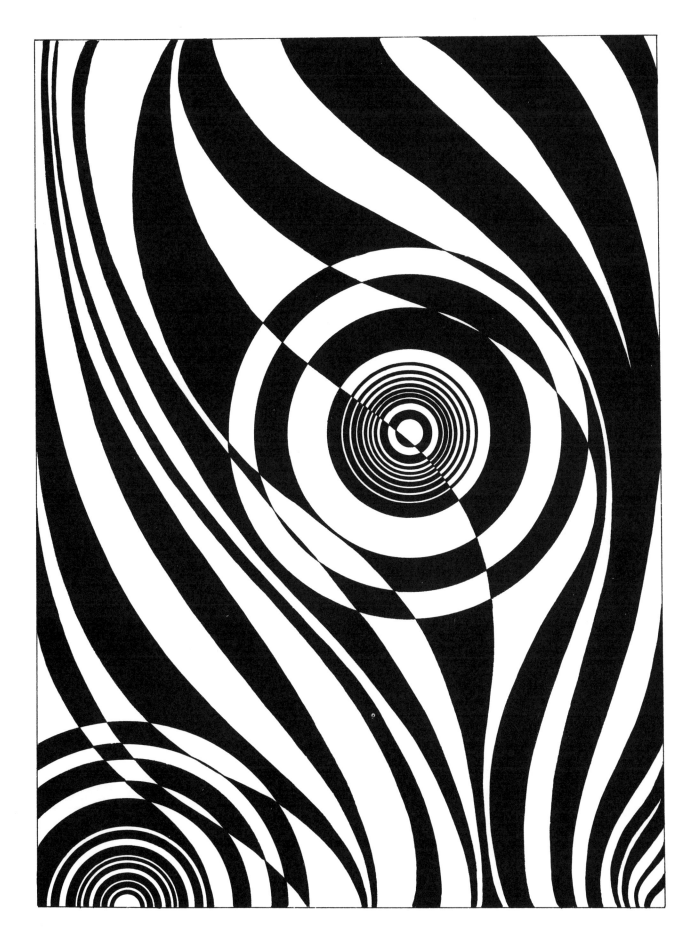

op art geometrics / PLATE 69

Conversationals

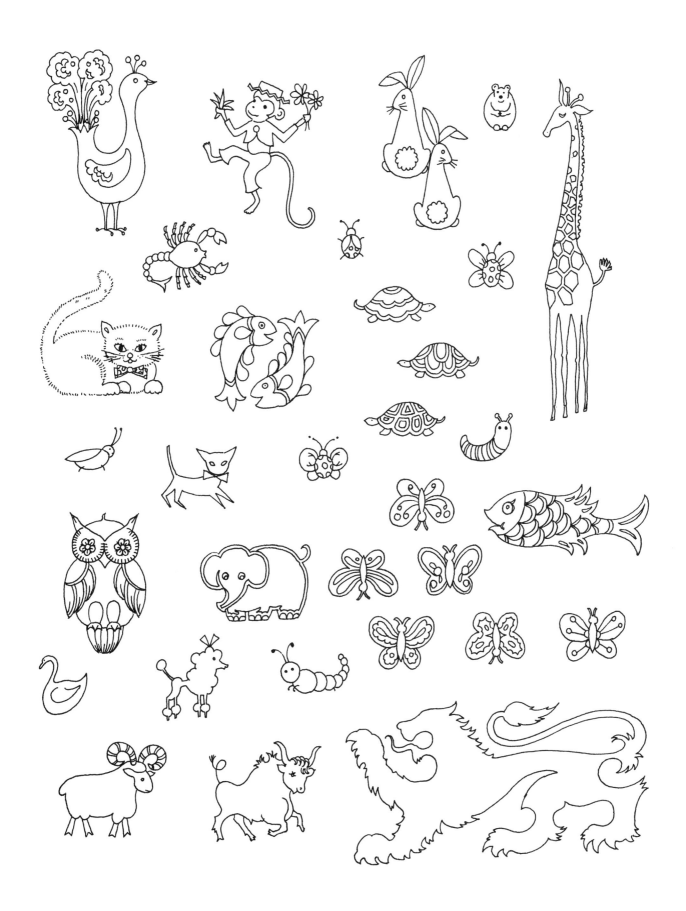

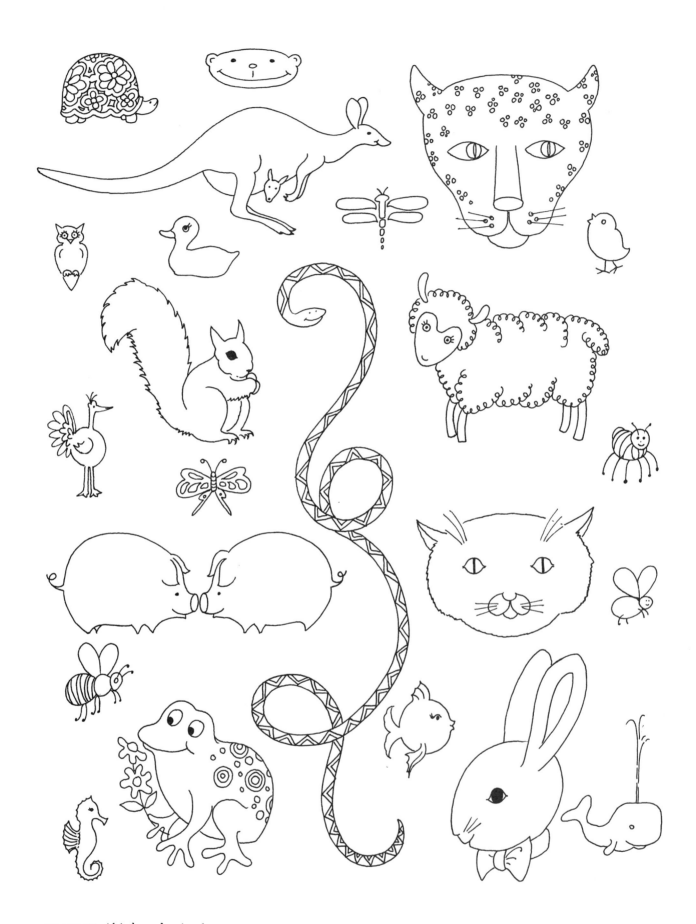

PLATE 71 / birds and animals

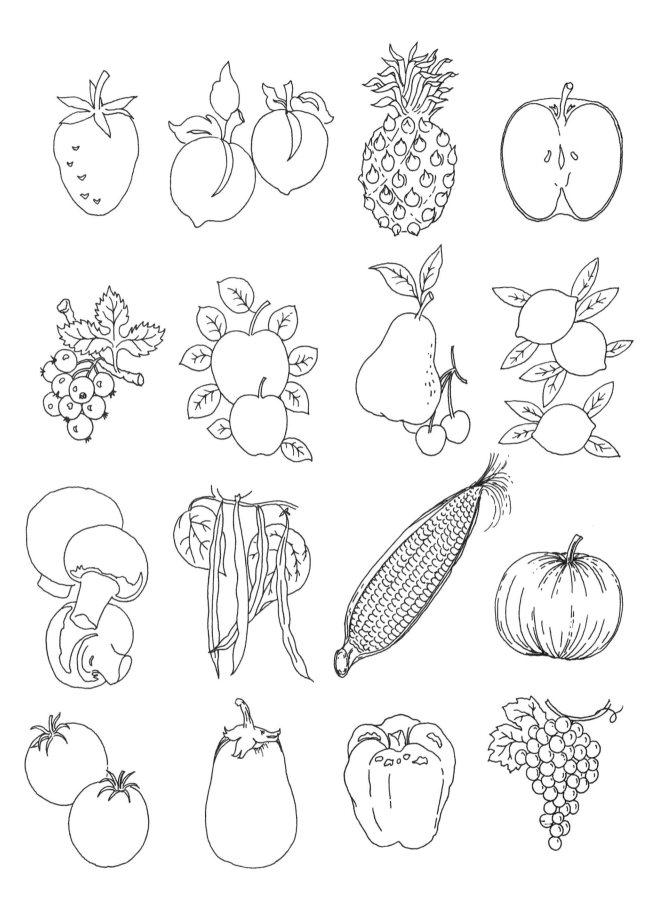

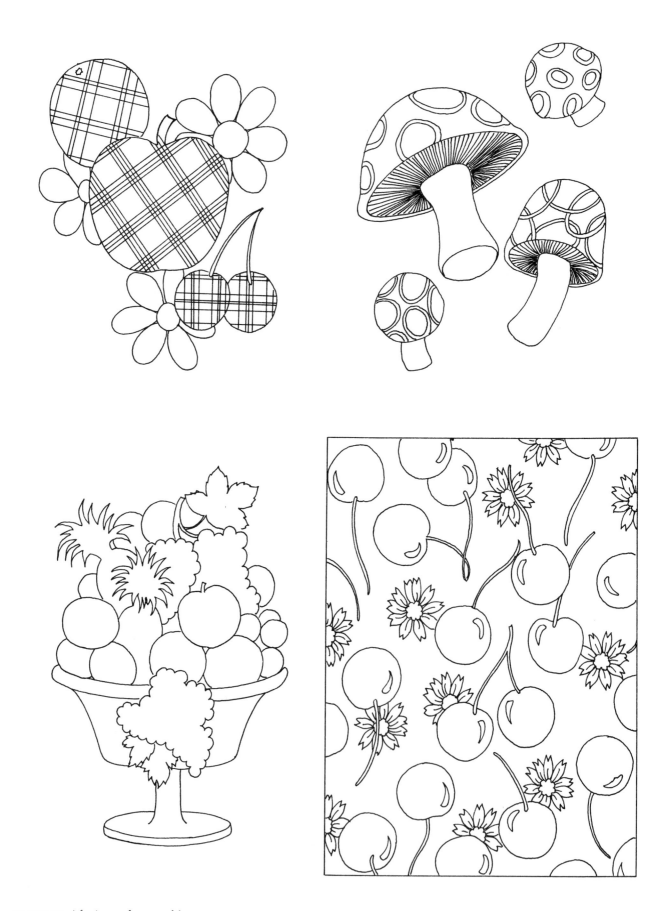

PLATE 73 / fruits and vegetables

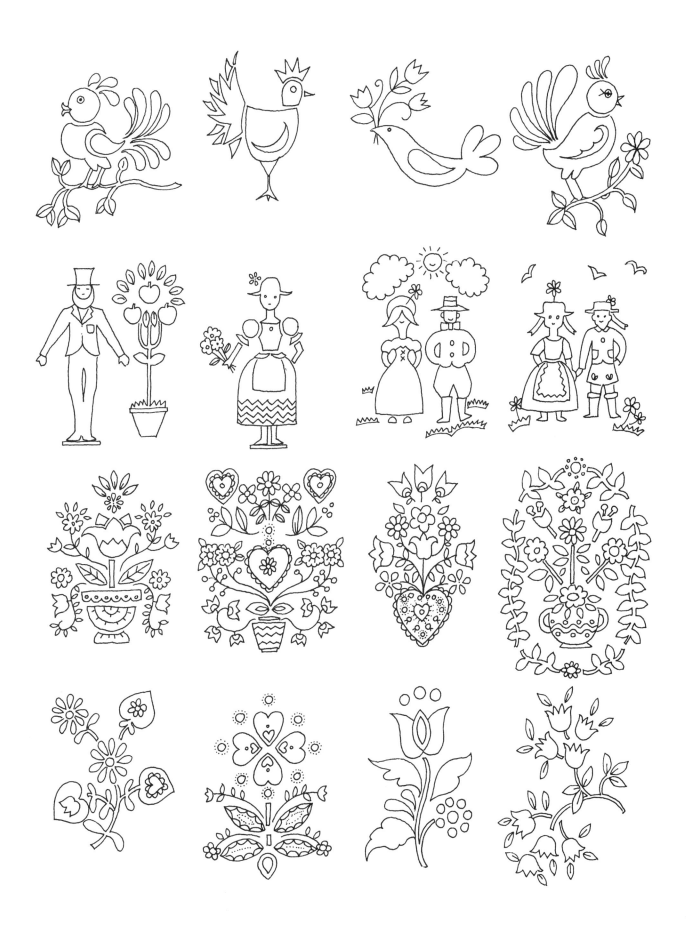

Tyrolean motifs / PLATE 74

PLATE 75 / Tyrolean motifs

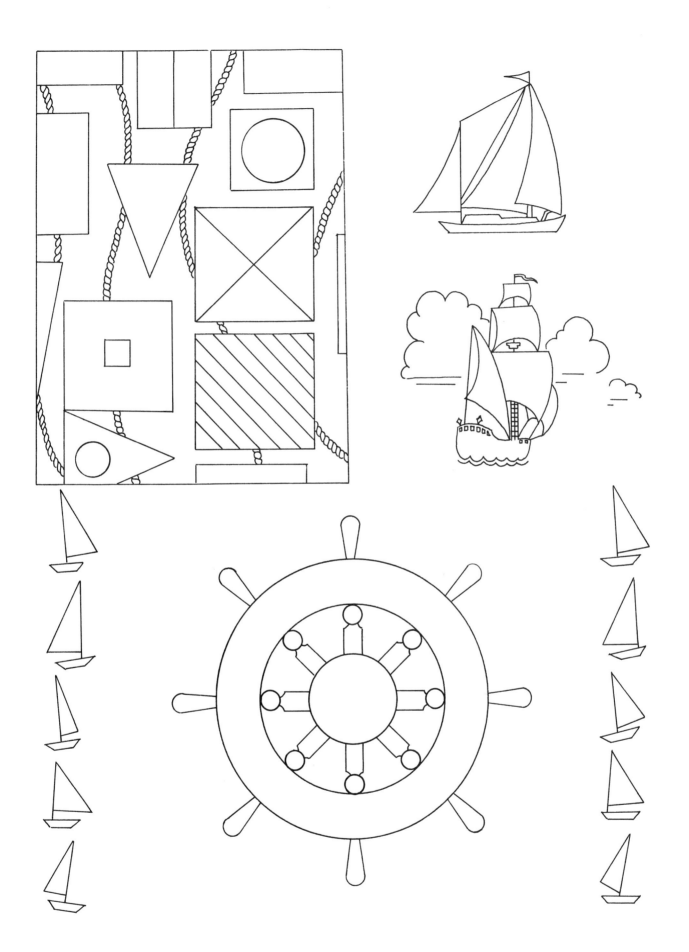

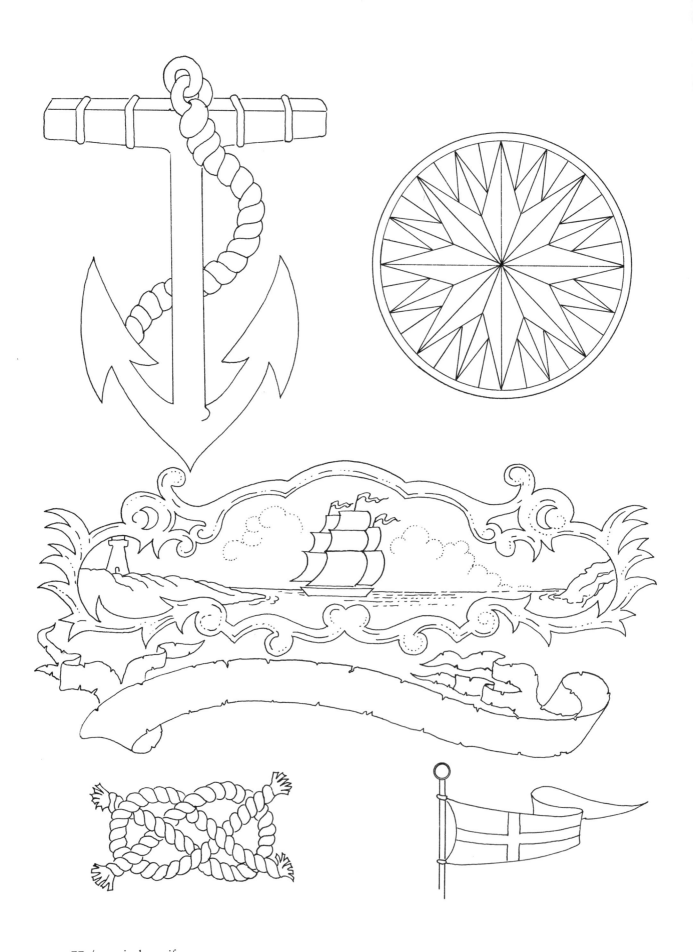

PLATE 77 / nautical motifs

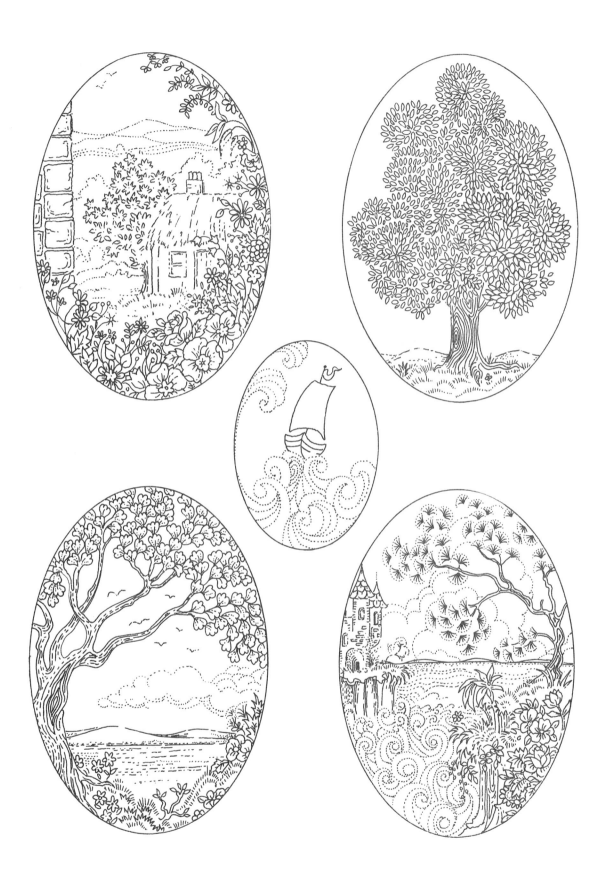

Folk Designs

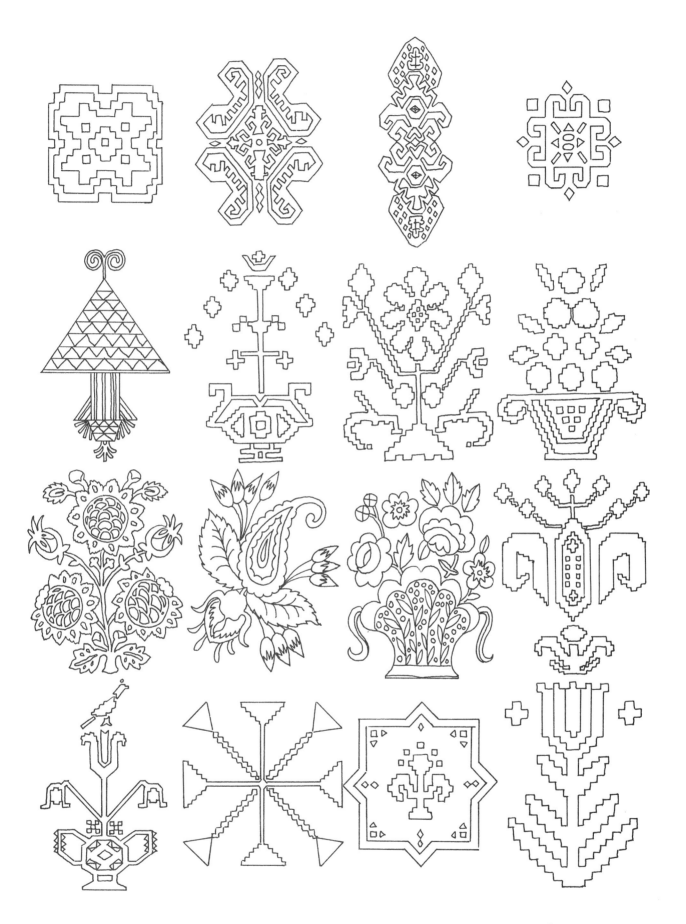

PLATE 80 / Scandinavian designs

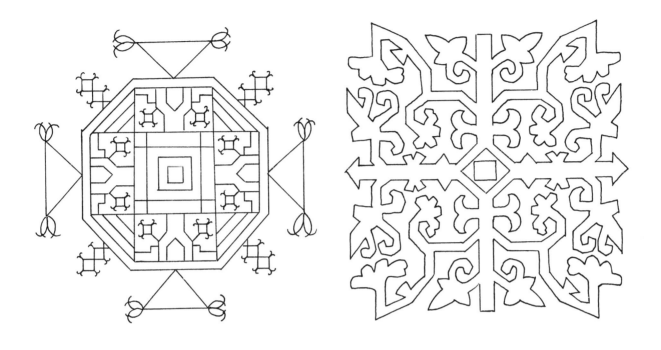

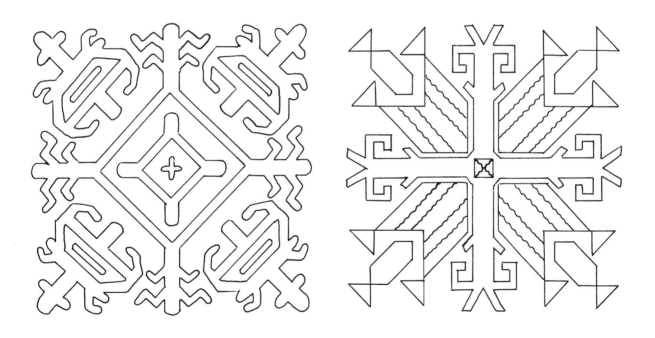

Slavic designs / PLATE 81

PLATE 82 / Slavic designs

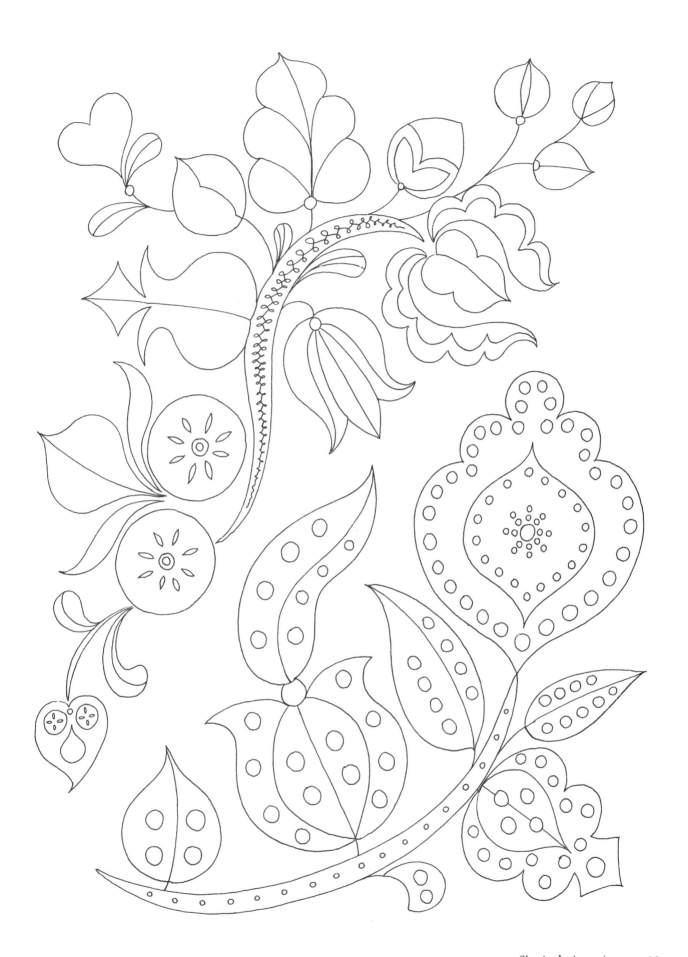

Slavic designs / PLATE 83

PLATE 84 / Mexican designs

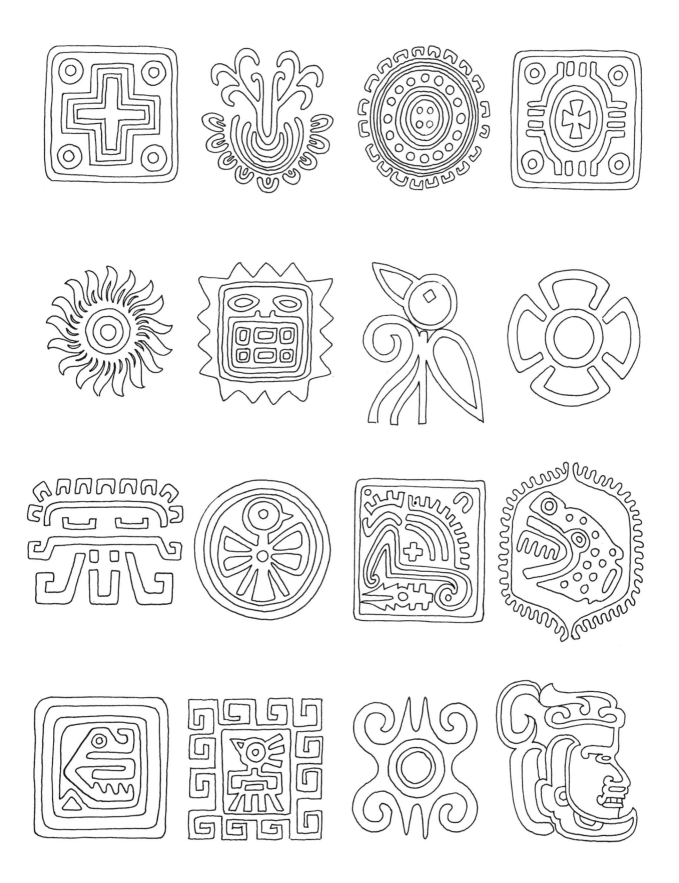

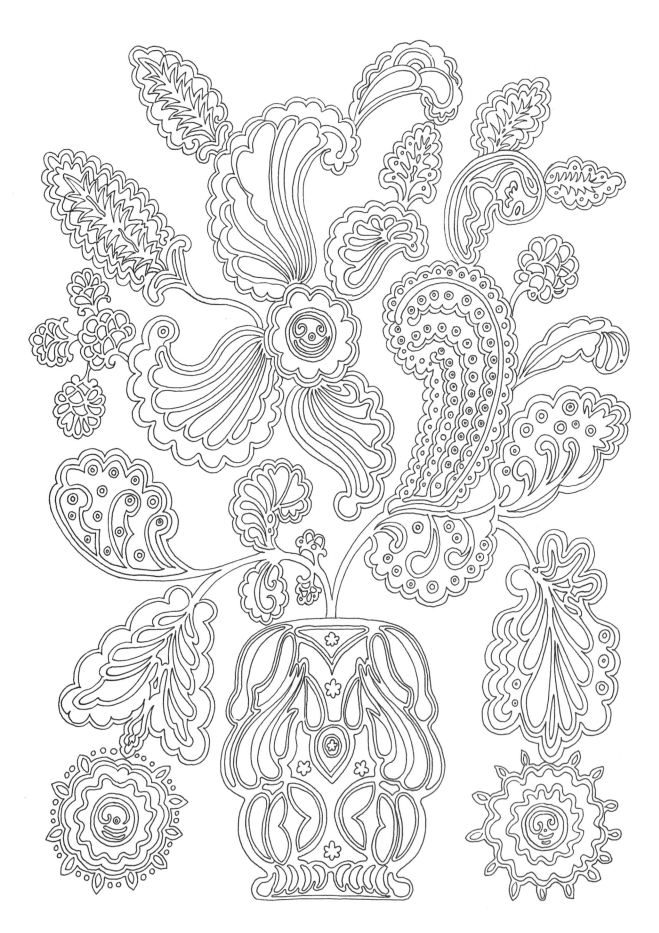

PLATE 86 / Mexican designs

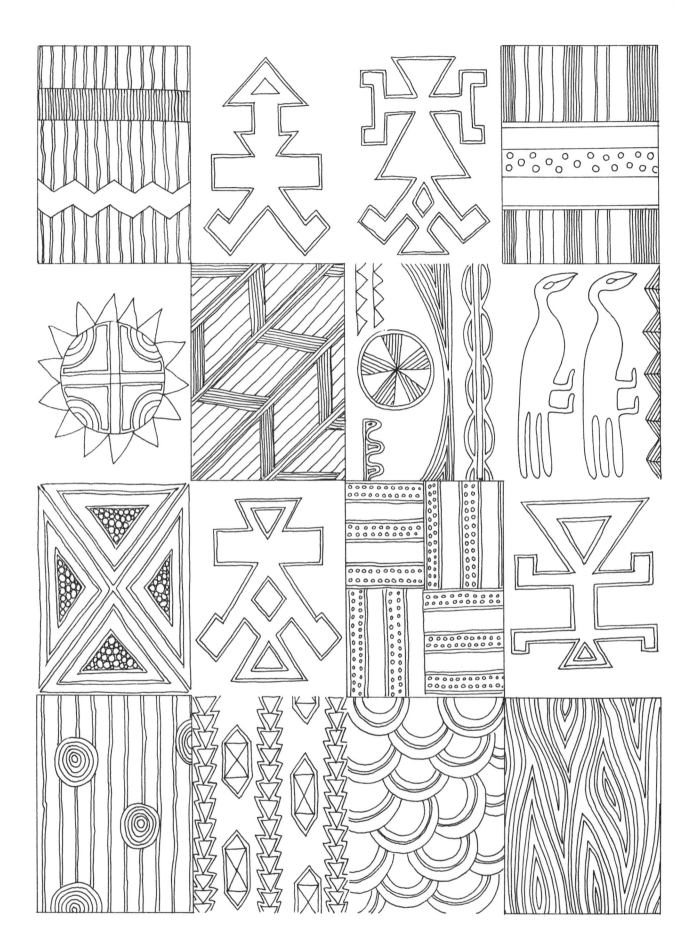

PLATE 88 / African designs

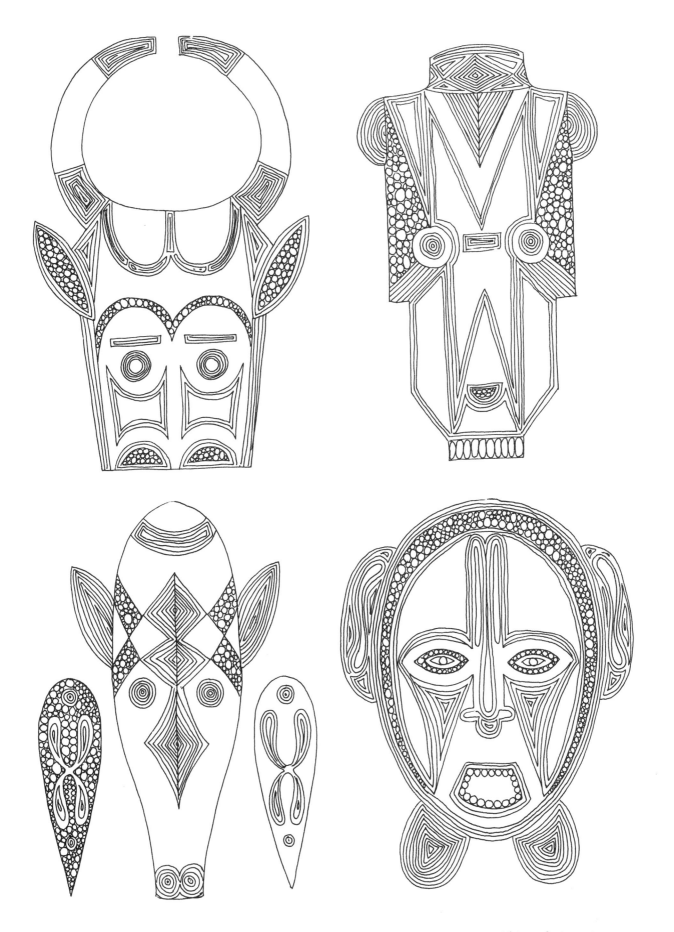

African designs / PLATE 89

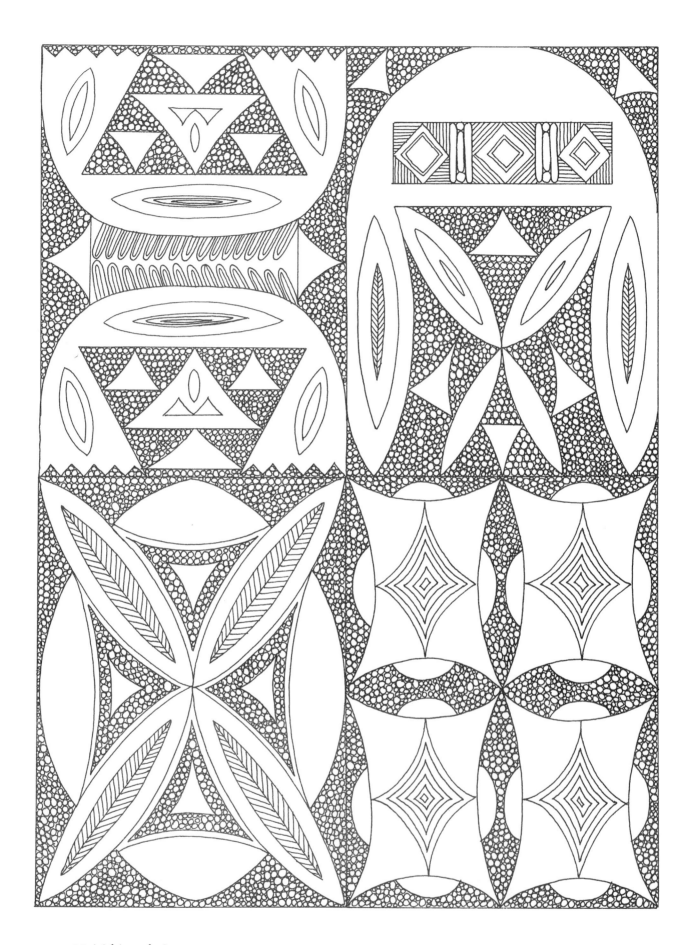

PLATE 90 / African designs

African designs / PLATE 91

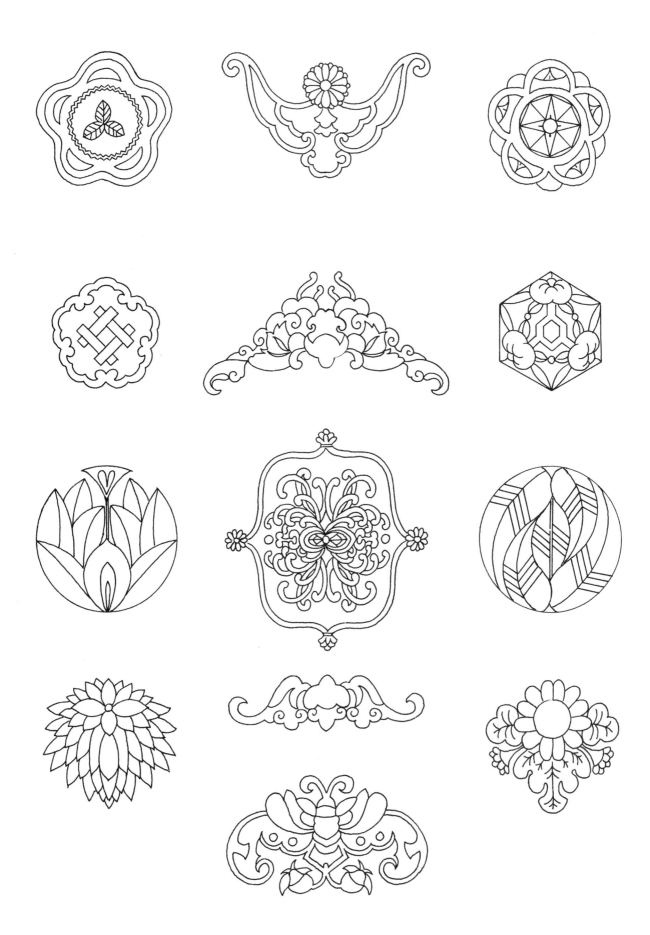

PLATE 92 / Oriental designs

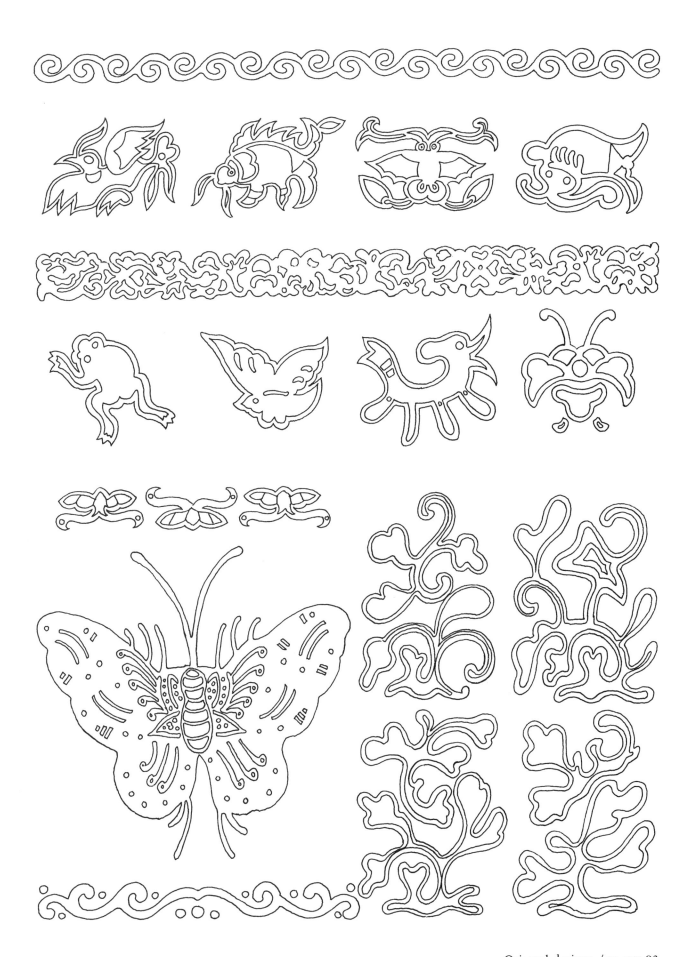

Oriental designs / PLATE 93

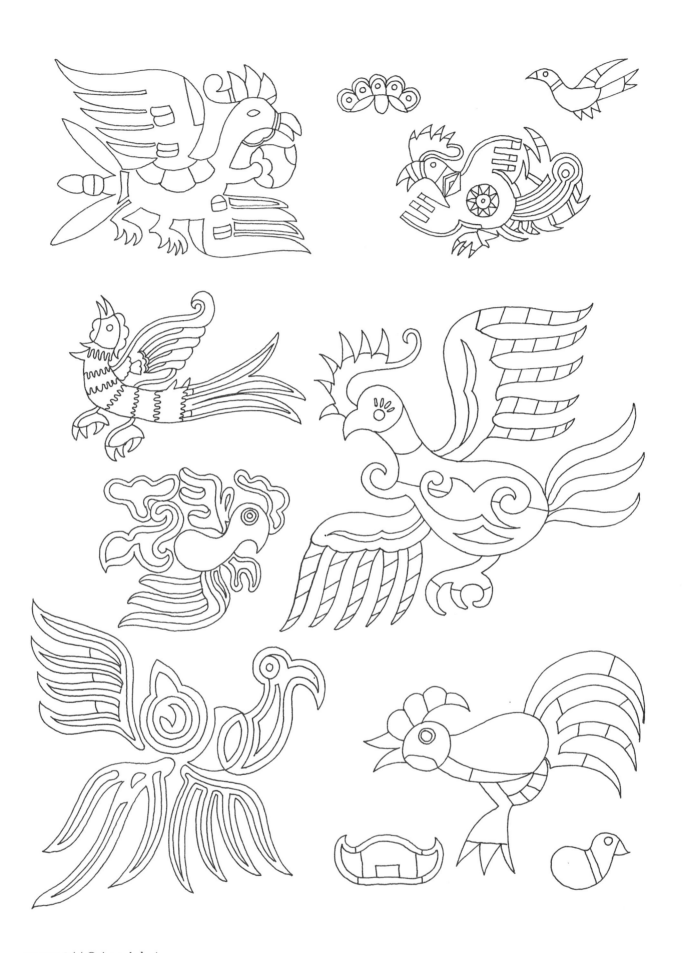

PLATE 94/ Oriental designs

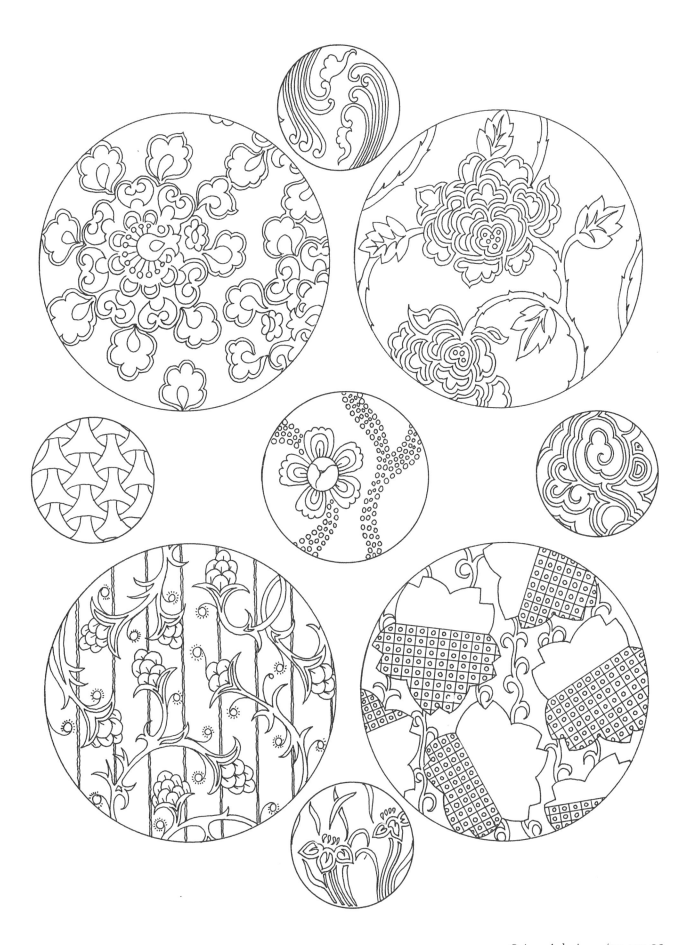

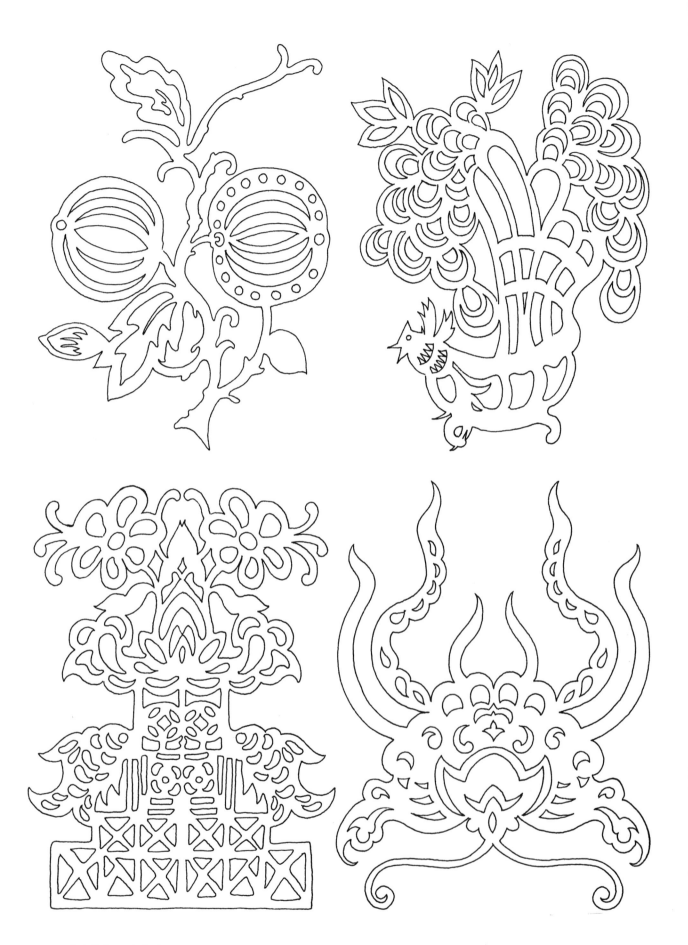

PLATE 96 / Oriental designs

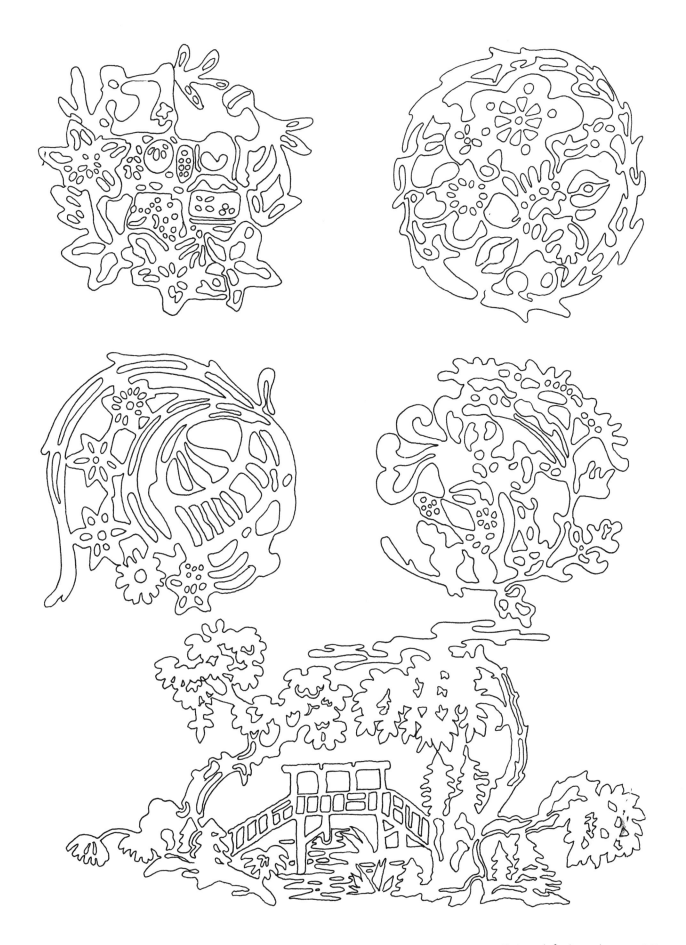

Oriental designs / PLATE 97

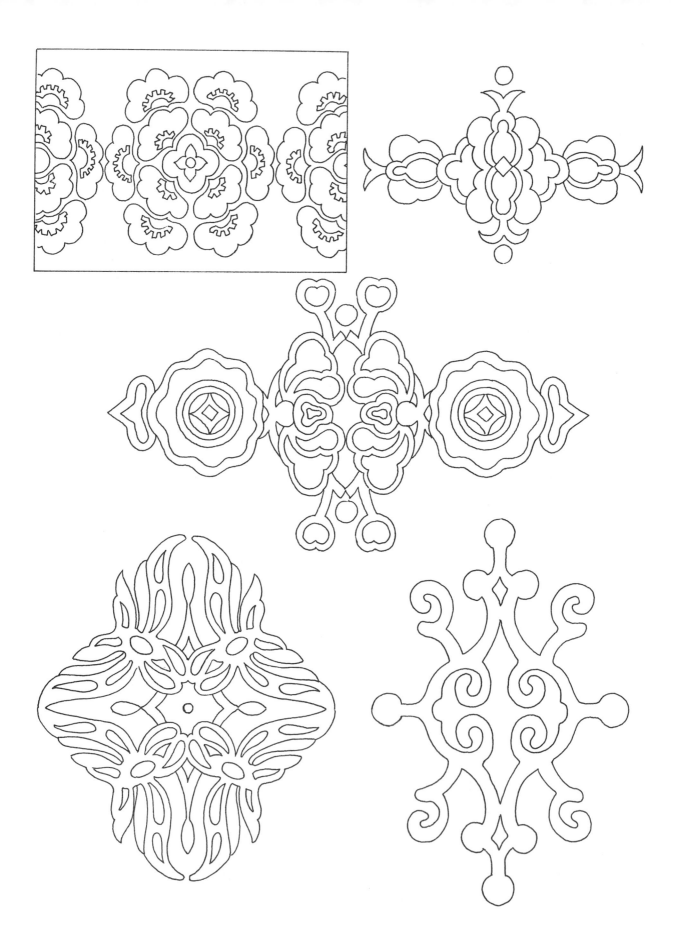

PLATE 98 / Oriental designs

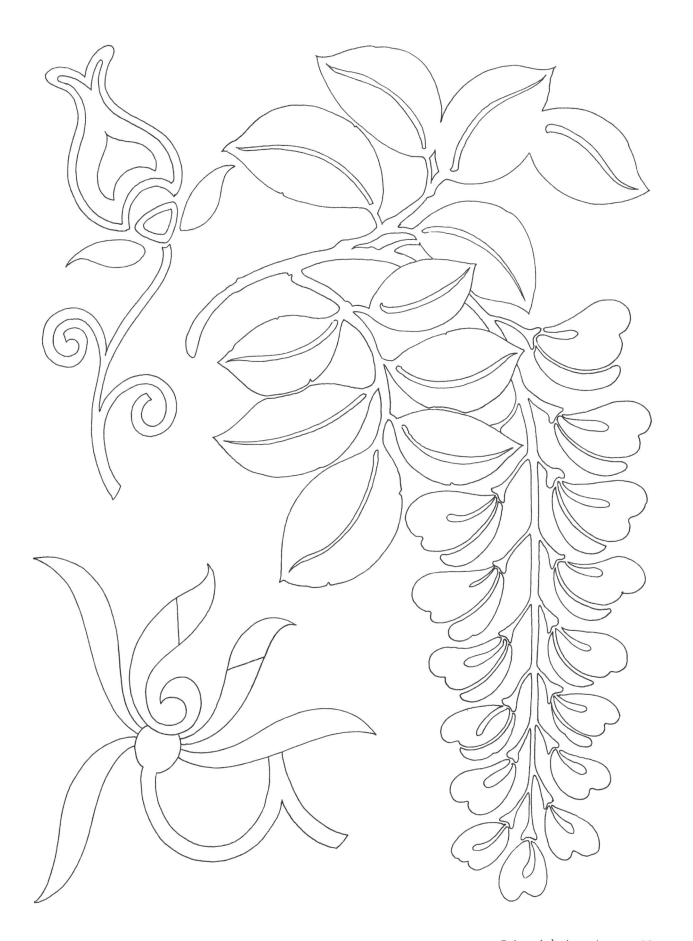

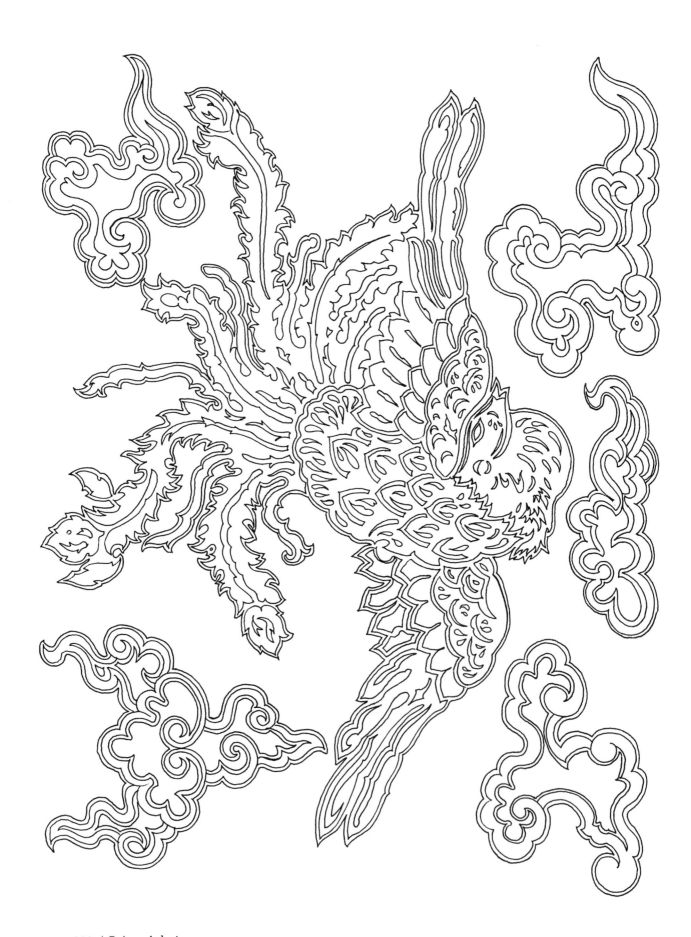

PLATE 100 / Oriental designs

Dover Books on Art

200 DECORATIVE TITLE-PAGES, edited by A. Nesbitt. Fascinating and informative from a historical point of view, this beautiful collection of decorated titles will be a great inspiration to students of design, commercial artists, advertising designers, etc. A complete survey of the genre from the first known decorated title to work in the first decades of this century. Bibliography and sources of the plates. 222pp. 8⅜ x 11¼.

21264-5 Paperbound $6.00

ON THE LAWS OF JAPANESE PAINTING, H. P. Bowie. This classic work on the philosophy and technique of Japanese art is based on the author's first-hand experiences studying art in Japan. Every aspect of Japanese painting is described: the use of the brush and other materials; laws governing conception and execution; subjects for Japanese paintings, etc. The best possible substitute for a series of lessons from a great Oriental master. Index. xv + 117pp. + 66 plates. 6⅛ x 9¼.

20030-2 Paperbound $5.00

A HANDBOOK OF ANATOMY FOR ART STUDENTS, Arthur Thomson. This long-popular text teaches any student, regardless of level of technical competence, all the subtleties of human anatomy. Clear photographs, numerous line sketches and diagrams of bones, joints, etc. Use it as a text for home study, as a supplement to life class work, or as a lifelong sourcebook and reference volume. Author's prefaces. 67 plates, containing 40 line drawings, 86 photographs—mostly full page. 211 figures. Appendix. Index. xx + 459pp. 5⅜ x 8⅜. 21163-0 Paperbound $5.00

WHITTLING AND WOODCARVING, E. J. Tangerman. With this book, a beginner who is moderately handy can whittle or carve scores of useful objects, toys for children, gifts, or simply pass hours creatively and enjoyably. "Easy as well as instructive reading," N. Y. Herald Tribune Books. 464 illustrations, with appendix and index. x + 293pp. 5½ x 8⅛.

20965-2 Paperbound $3.50

ONE HUNDRED AND ONE PATCHWORK PATTERNS, Ruby Short McKim. Whether you have made a hundred quilts or none at all, you will find this the single most useful book on quilt-making. There are 101 full patterns (all exact size) with full instructions for cutting and sewing. In addition there is some really choice folklore about the origin of the ingenious pattern names: "Monkey Wrench," "Road to California," "Drunkard's Path," "Crossed Canoes," to name a few. Over 500 illustrations. 124 pp. 7⅞ x 10¾. 20773-0 Paperbound $3.25

ART AND GEOMETRY, W. M. Ivins, Jr. Challenges the idea that the foundations of modern thought were laid in ancient Greece. Pitting Greek tactile-muscular intuitions of space against modern visual intuitions, the author, for 30 years curator of prints, Metropolitan Museum of Art, analyzes the differences between ancient and Renaissance painting and sculpture and tells of the first fruitful investigations of perspective. x + 113pp. 5⅜ x 8⅜. 20941-5 Paperbound $2.50

Dover Books on Art

PENNSYLVANIA DUTCH AMERICAN FOLK ART, H. J. Kauffman. The originality and charm of this early folk art give it a special appeal even today, and surviving pieces are sought by collectors all over the country. Here is a rewarding introductory guide to the Dutch country and its household art, concentrating on pictorial matter—hex signs, tulip ware, weather vanes, interiors, paintings and folk sculpture, rocking horses and children's toys, utensils, Stiegel-type glassware, etc. "A serious, worthy and helpful volume," W. G. Dooley, N. Y. TIMES. Introduction. Bibliography. 279 halftone illustrations. 28 motifs and other line drawings. 1 map. 146pp. 7⅞ x 10¾.

21205-X Paperbound $4.00

DESIGN AND EXPRESSION IN THE VISUAL ARTS, J. F. A. Taylor. Here is a much needed discussion of art theory which relates the new and sometimes bewildering directions of 20th century art to the great traditions of the past. The first discussion of principle that addresses itself to the eye rather than to the intellect, using illustrations from Rembrandt, Leonardo, Mondrian, El Greco, etc. List of plates. Index. 59 reproductions. 5 color plates. 75 figures. x + 245pp. 5⅜ x 8½.

21195-9 Paperbound $3.50

THE ENJOYMENT AND USE OF COLOR, W. Sargent. Requiring no special technical know-how, this book tells you all about color and how it is created, perceived, and imitated in art. Covers many little-known facts about color values, intensities, effects of high and low illumination, complementary colors, and color harmonies. Simple do-it-yourself experiments and observations. 35 illustrations, including 6 full-page color plates. New color frontispiece. Index. x + 274 pp. 5⅜ x 8.

20944-X Paperbound $3.50

STYLES IN PAINTING, Paul Zucker. By comparing paintings of similar subject matter, the author shows the characteristics of various painting styles. You are shown at a glance the differences between reclining nudes by Giorgione, Velasquez, Goya, Modigliani; how a Byzantine portrait is unlike a portrait by Van Eyck, da Vinci, Dürer, or Marc Chagall; how the painting of landscapes has changed gradually from ancient Pompeii to Lyonel Feininger in our own century. 241 beautiful, sharp photographs illustrate the text. xiv + 338 pp. 5⅝ x 8¼.

20760-9 Paperbound $4.00

Dover publishes books on commercial art, art history, crafts, design, art classics; also books on music, literature, science, mathematics, puzzles and entertainments, chess, engineering, biology, philosophy, psychology, languages, history, and other fields. For free circulars write to Dept. DA, Dover Publications, Inc., 180 Varick St., New York, N.Y. 10014.